GW01339580

LEARNING

PALMISTRY

ROBERTA PETERS

Published in 2001 by Caxton Editions
20 Bloomsbury Street
London WC1B 3JH
a member of the Caxton Publishing Group

© 2001 Caxton Publishing Group

Designed and produced for Caxton Editions
by Open Door Limited
Rutland, United Kingdom

Editing: Mary Morton
Digital imagery © PhotoDisc inc.
Colour separation: GA Graphics, Stamford

All rights reserved. No part of this publication may be reproduced or transmitted in any form or by any means, electronic or mechanical, including photocopying, recording or any information storage and retrieval system, without prior permission in writing from the copyright owner.

Title: Palmistry
ISBN: 1 84067 279 X

LEARNING
PALMISTRY

ROBERTA PETERS

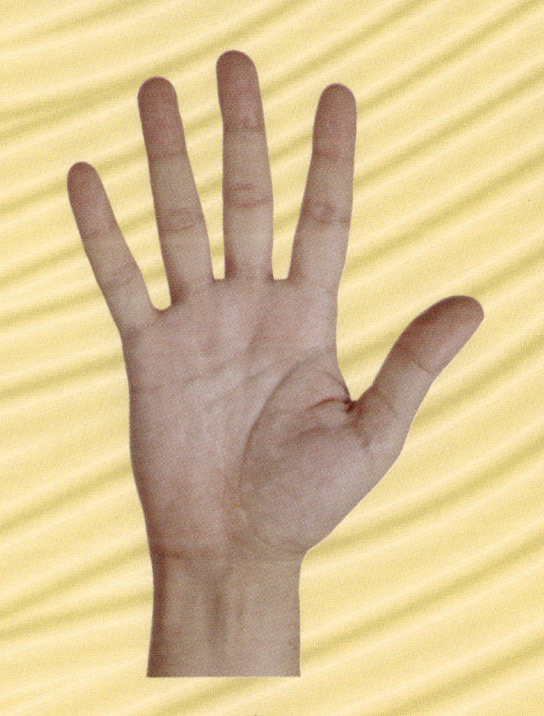

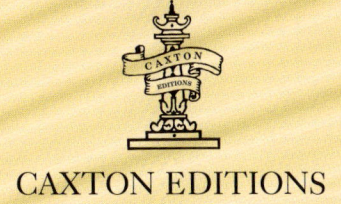

CAXTON EDITIONS

CONTENTS

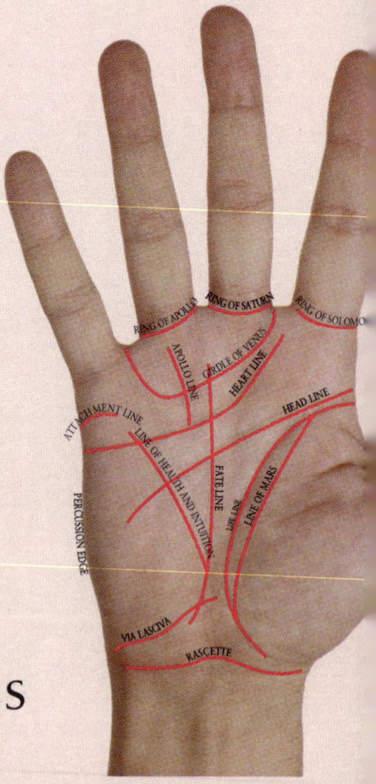

6   INTRODUCTION

8   SECRETS ON DISPLAY

16   ALL FINGERS AND THUMBS

24   GETTING AROUND THE HAND

32   WHAT THE LINES CAN TELL

53   LOVE, PARTNERSHIP AND FAMILY

CONTENTS

64 FATE, FORTUNE AND FAME

76 MARKS AND LOOPS

84 HEALTH ON THE HANDS

90 HOW TO MAKE HAND PRINTS

94 INDEX

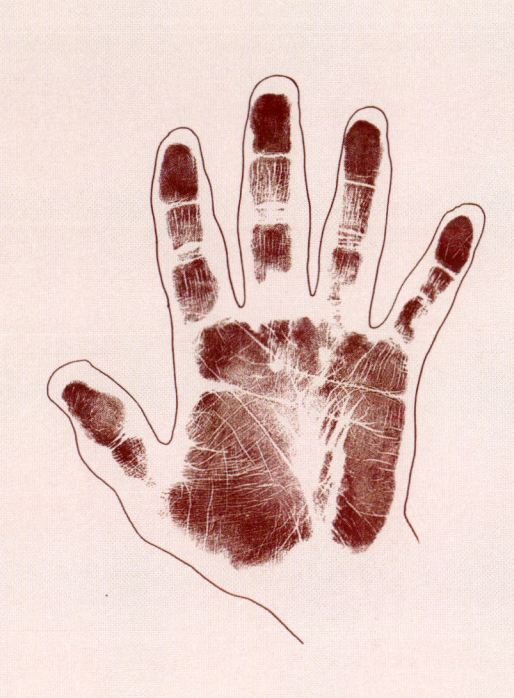

INTRODUCTION

"Length of her days is in her right hand; and in her left hand riches and honour."
Proverbs ch. 3, v. 16

This quote from the Bible shows just how old the study of palmistry is. The woman in the quotation is not a real person but an archetype for wisdom which may hark back to paganism. Having said that, "wisdom" must be left-handed, for only a very left-handed person would show the general trend of life in the right hand with worldly goods and success shown in the left!

Judging by the cave paintings of hands that have been left by stone age people, humans have been studying their hands for a very long time. Pythagoras and other ancient Greeks wrote about this as far back as 497 BC and they may have picked up their information from gypsies and others who came from the east. Today, hand reading is widely practiced all over the world and particularly so in Asia and the Orient. Napoleon Bonaparte was fascinated by all forms of divination, so he and his colleagues gathered information while travelling in Egypt, Spain and Eastern Europe during the Napoleonic wars. This may have encouraged a number of 19th-century investigators to look into the subject, or it may have just been a coincidence that much modern palmistry originated in France. The first books on scientific palmistry were French and the most famous of these were *Cheiro's Guide to the Hand* and *Language of the Hand* which were written by Count Louis Hamon, who was better known by his pen name "Cheiro". Incidentally, this name is pronounced kyro and not cheerio as I have heard some pronounce it.

Right: hands have fascinated mankind and been studied by them for thousands of years.

INTRODUCTION

There are various styles of hand reading in use today. Clairvoyants will peer at a client's hand as a means of tuning in. At the other end of the scale, there are "scientific" palmists who only study the lines, marks, shapes, mounts and so on. Naturally, there are many clairvoyants who use scientific knowledge and many scientific readers who use psychic ability. Some Indian and Chinese palmists read not only the lines but also use random marks and day-to-day patches of discoloration as a means of assessing a client's state of mind or his situation at the time of a reading. There is a certain amount of agreement among palmists the world over about the main aspects of hand reading, but individual palmists use a variety of interpretations for the less common lines.

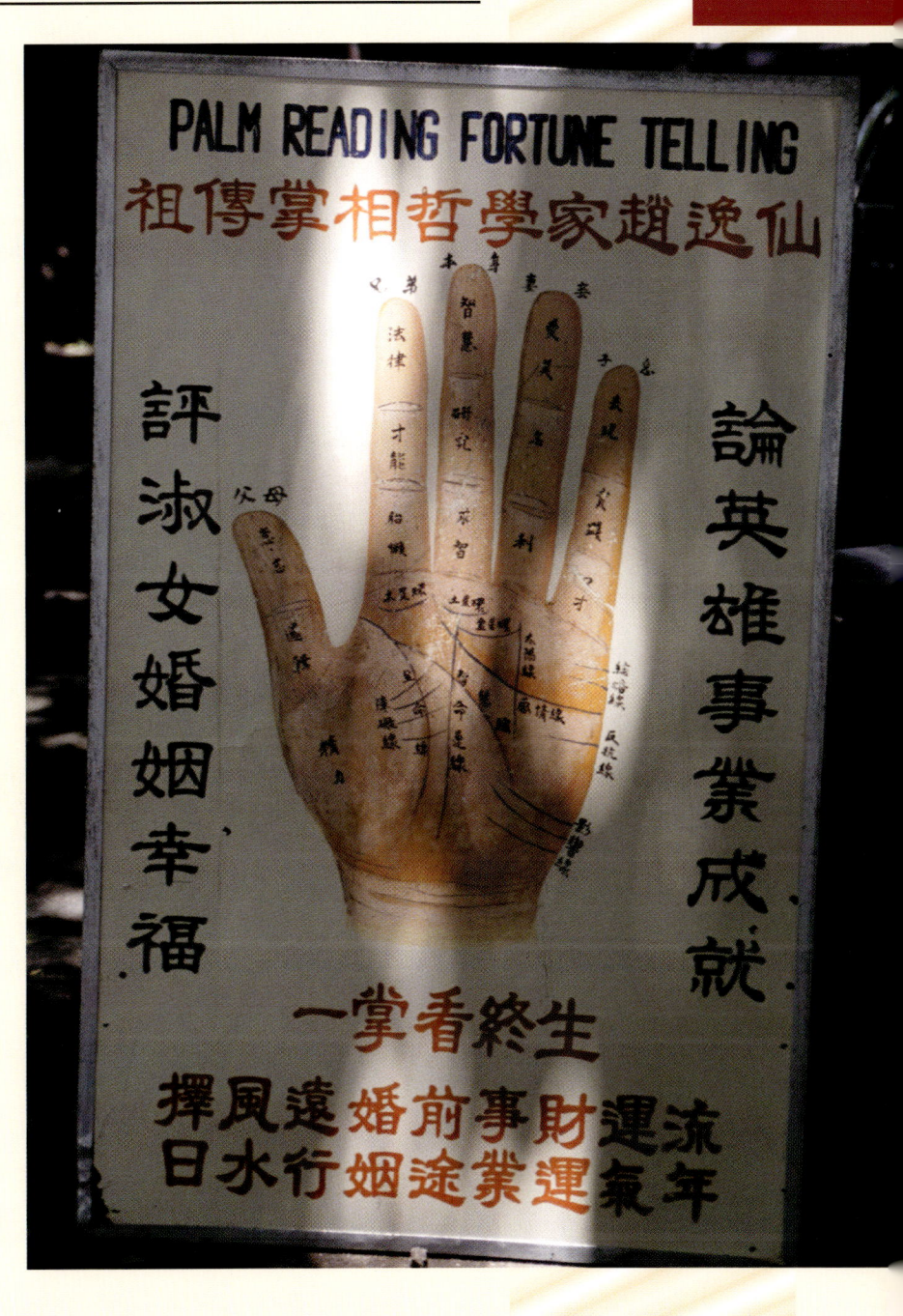

In a book like this, I can give you enough information to read a person's hands in a basic way, but if you want to become a professional you will need to study many hands over a period of years.

Above: a Chinese palmistry sign. The Chinese study not only the lines on a hand but also patches of discoloration.

Secrets on Display

A friend of mine once worked for a recruitment consultancy and part of her job was to interview men for tough engineering work in overseas locations. Specially qualified people made the final selections, but my pal did the initial interviews. Her bosses were frequently astounded by the accuracy of her character assessments and they wondered how she managed to pick up so quickly on personality traits that showed one man to be exactly right for a certain job, and another exactly wrong. What they didn't realise was that she had a high level of scientific hand-reading skill. Neither my friend's bosses nor the interviewees could have guessed that a clever hand reader can tell a great deal about a person, even when that person has no idea that their hands are being observed.

Right: a clever hand reader can tell a great deal about a person by studying their hands even when they are not aware that they are being observed.

SECRETS ON DISPLAY

LEFT AND RIGHT HANDS

A frequently asked question is "which hand do you read?" The answer is that we read both hands. Science tells us that about 90 per cent of the population is right-handed, but in reality many people are a bit of each, and left-handed people are often fairly ambidextrous because of having to live in a right-handed world. Palmists usually consider the hand that someone writes with to be the dominant one. We call this the major hand and the less dominant one the minor hand. The minor hand is more concerned with the inner personality. The major hand shows how a person adapts to the world and how he experiences life. The minor hand leans more towards emotional matters and private life, so it has much to say about love, family matters, emotions and health issues. The major hand has more bearing on the practical issues of work, finances, property matters, travel, the outer personality and the way a person adapts to his circumstances.

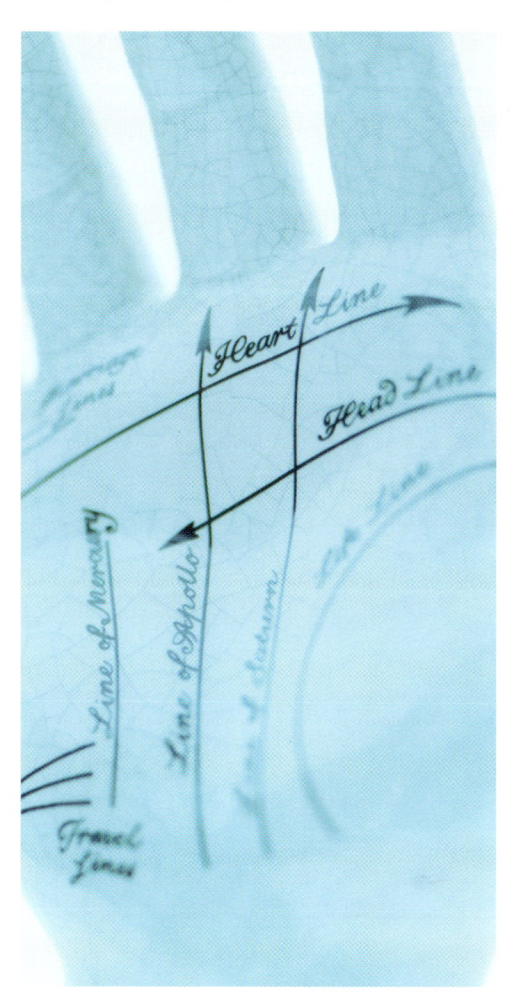

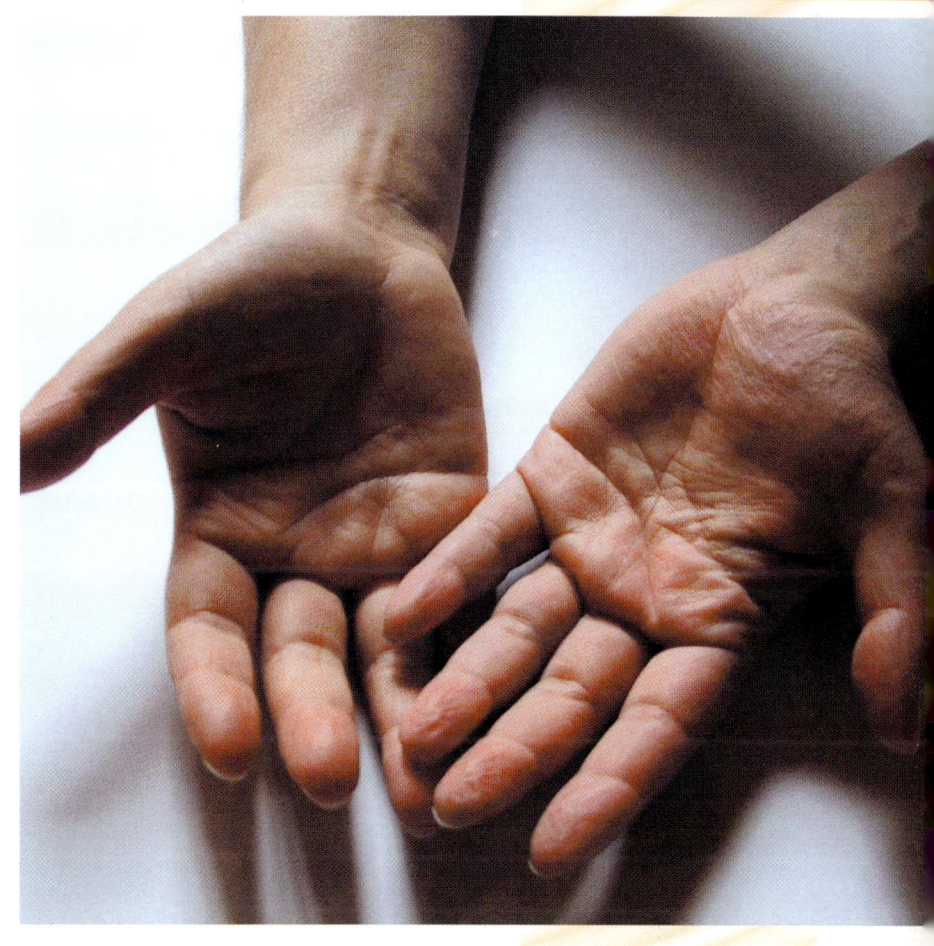

Unfortunately, this division is frequently not clear cut, so it is always wise to look at both hands. Some say that the minor hand looks backwards and the major one looks forwards, and it is true that past traumas show up more fully on the minor hand than the major one.

Above: both the left and the right hands can be read.

Left: The major hand, whether left or right, has more bearing on the practical issues of life than the minor one does.

SECRETS ON DISPLAY

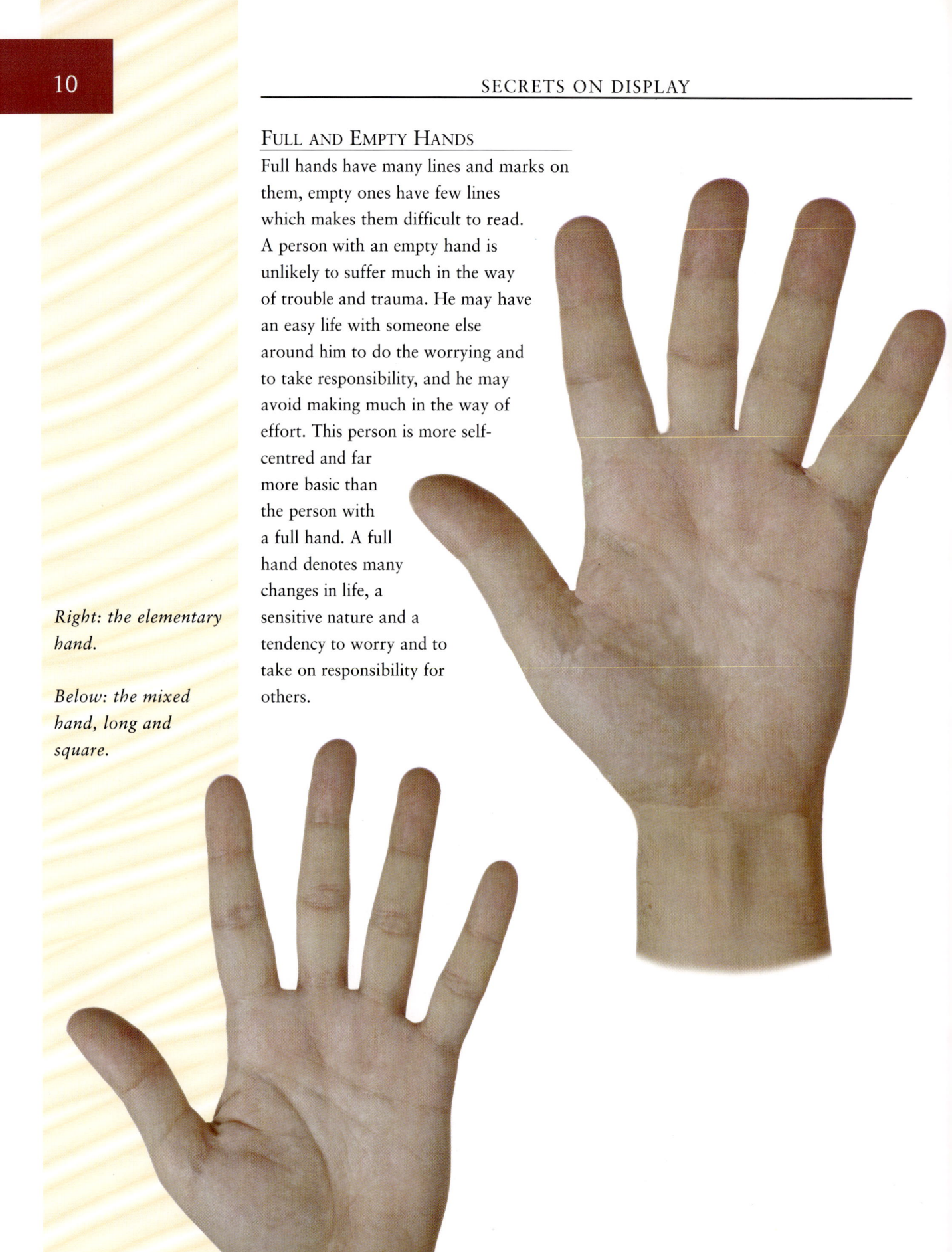

FULL AND EMPTY HANDS

Full hands have many lines and marks on them, empty ones have few lines which makes them difficult to read. A person with an empty hand is unlikely to suffer much in the way of trouble and trauma. He may have an easy life with someone else around him to do the worrying and to take responsibility, and he may avoid making much in the way of effort. This person is more self-centred and far more basic than the person with a full hand. A full hand denotes many changes in life, a sensitive nature and a tendency to worry and to take on responsibility for others.

Right: the elementary hand.

Below: the mixed hand, long and square.

SECRETS ON DISPLAY

HAND SHAPES

Cheiro suggested that there were seven hand shapes and he called them:

The elementary, or the lowest type.

The square, or the useful hand.

The spatulate, or the active, nervous type.

The philosophic, or the knotty hand.

The conic, or the artistic type.

The psychic, or the idealistic hand.

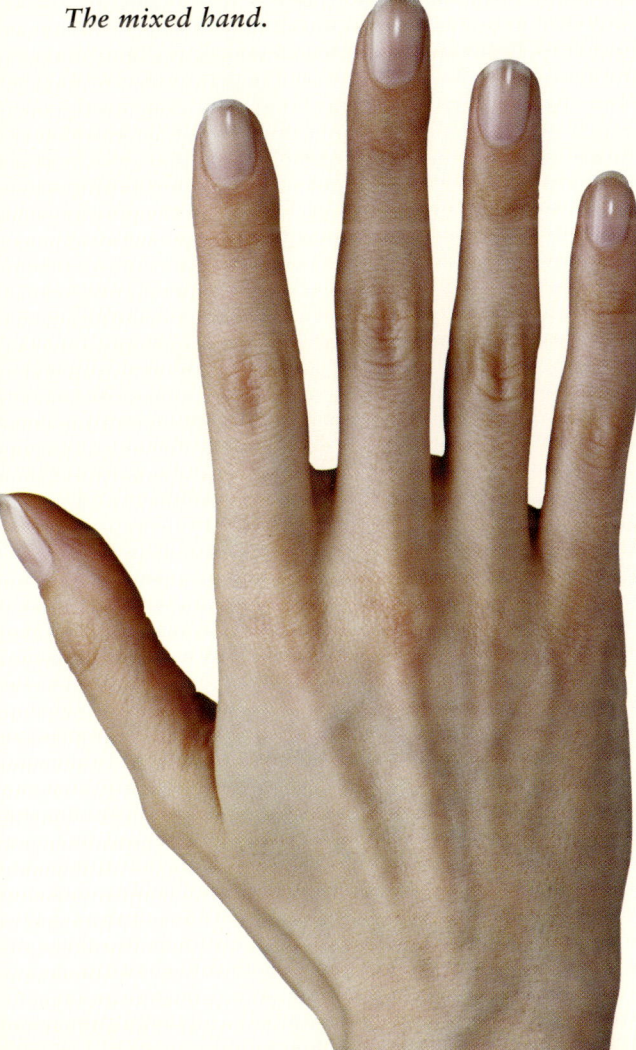

The mixed hand.

When a beginner tries to work out which category a hand that he is looking at belongs to, he immediately gets into a muddle, so I suggest that you keep things simple. The only truly elementary hands belong to those who have Down's Syndrome or other similar disabilities. Other hands with an unformed or unfinished look belong to those who have a basic outlook on life or who never really grow up. Square hands denote practicality while long hands suggest a more artistic and sensitive nature.

Above: the square hand.

Left: the psychic hand.

SECRETS ON DISPLAY

Right: the philosophic hand.

Below: the spatulate hand.

Knobbly hands with knotty knuckles belong to those who enjoy using their brains and who may be introverted, shy and slow to take action. These people may be loners or a little choosy about those who they call friends. Rounded hands denote sociability but rounded hands that are soft or fatty suggest laziness. Small hands denote energy and speed of action, while large hands often belong to a slow-moving type of person. Smooth hands signify a more refined and sensitive nature than rough ones. Smooth fingers suggest less time spent thinking before acting.

If the palm and the fingers don't match up, the personality is mixed, being partly practical and responsible and partly dreamy, artistic or flighty. A square palm will add practicality to a creative or psychic nature. If the fingers are long and slender, this person may find some tasks easier to dream about than to achieve. Conversely, a longer palm allied to shortish fingers allows a creative person to complete artistic or creative tasks in a practical way.

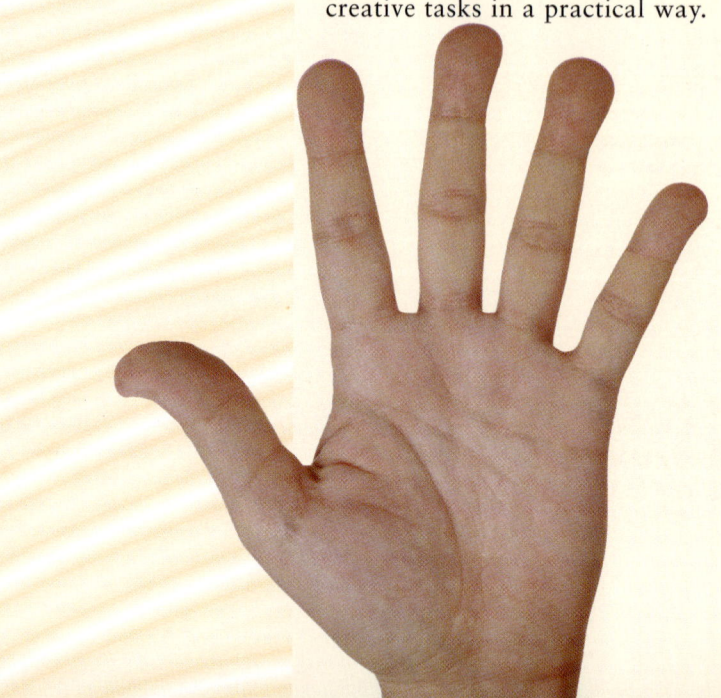

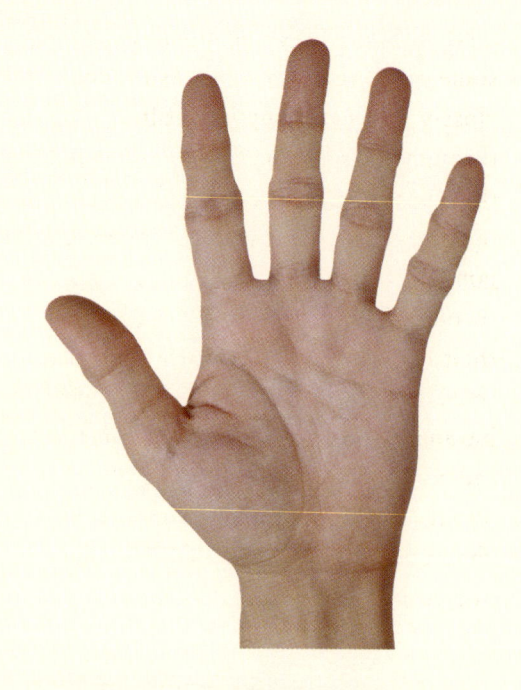

Next time you are watching a drama on television, take a look at the actors' hands. The chances are that they will have fairly large hands with long fingers and the index, middle and ring finger may appear to be almost all the same length. If the actor is a particularly athletic person, the hands have a strong appearance with a prominent knuckle at the base of the thumb; the ball of the thumb will be flexible and able to turn outwards from the hand. Those who put on an act for a living, such as salesmen and women, also have such hands. A flexible hand suggests impulsiveness and a person who can pick themselves up at a moment's notice and move to the other side of the world. People whose thumbs turn back at the tip go into a shop to buy one thing and come out with something completely different – and far more expensive!

SECRETS ON DISPLAY

Next time you watch a politician or some other pundit on television, look closely and see if any light filters through their fingers while they make their points. If it does, then they are open to reason, but if their fingers are jammed together so that no light shows through they are only interested in their own opinions. This is even more the case when you notice a politician haranguing the audience with their index finger pointing or wagging about. Two such politicians with this characteristic are Margaret Thatcher and Anne Widdecombe.

Nurses and those who care for others often have flexible fingertips that turn back easily. Such people can cope with shift work while those whose fingers are more rigid prefer a job with regular hours.

If a hand looks meaty with hard-packed flesh, the person could be a bully or merely a hard worker. However, if the percussion edge of the hand bows out in a thick fat curve the subject won't be able to control his temper. Don't expect a person with soft, flabby hands to help out in a crisis – or indeed at any other time either. Fat little hands with pointed fingertips and curved finger nails indicate self-centredness and a sharp tongue. Square palms or square hands belong to a survivor.

Below left: politicians who have their fingers tightly closed tend to be interested only in their own opinions.

Below: nurses and those who care for others often have flexible fingertips that turn back easily.

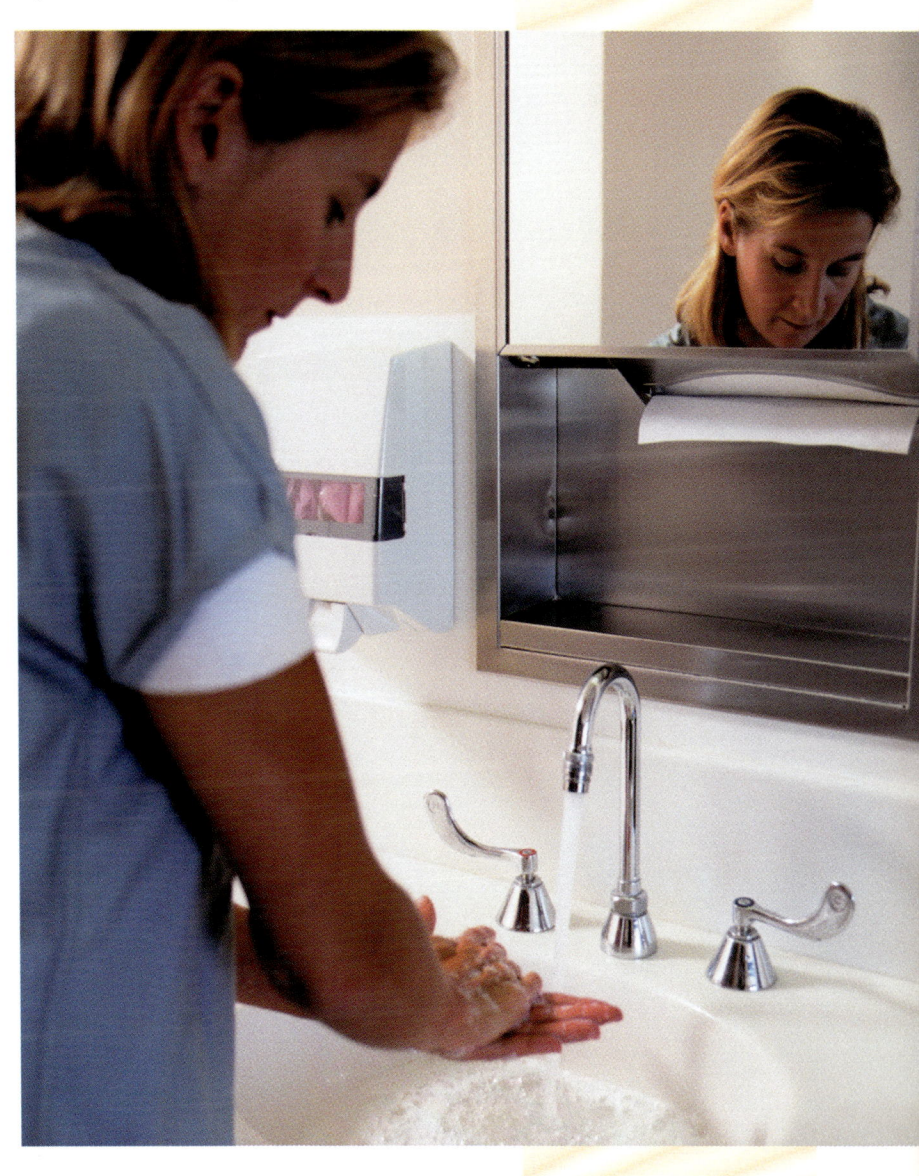

SECRETS ON DISPLAY

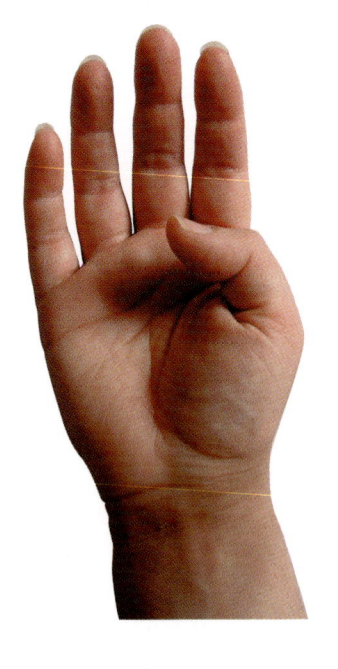

Above right: a suspicious and wary person's thumb falls across the palm when the shake test is performed.

Right: if the thumb remains at the side of the hand during the shake test then the subject is open and lacks suspicion.

THE SHAKE TEST

Ask a friend to relax his hands by shaking them vigorously and then to hold them up as if he was surrendering. If the thumbs stay at the side of the hands, your friend is quite open and lacks suspicion about the motives of others. If the thumb falls in front of the palm, he has a more secretive personality and he is suspicious and wary. However friendly your pal might be, there are areas of his life that he prefers to keep private. This person has had a difficult childhood and he learned early that it was a good policy to keep his opinions to himself.

A thumb that is set low and which opens at a 90-degree angle or more belongs to an open and sociable person who enjoys working and socialising among others. The thumb that is set higher on the hand and that remains close to the hand belongs to someone who needs a quiet life and who lives inside his own head to some extent. Such a person may prefer to work from home or in an environment that feels safe and where he can work on creative projects. A child who clutches his thumb in his fingers is frightened and unhappy. This may be a passing phase, but if it persists something is scaring the child stiff, and abuse should be considered.

If after shaking there is a gap between the forefinger and the middle finger, this shows a person with an independent mind. If the little finger falls away from the ring finger, the subject is slow to give his heart or his love to someone else. While on the subject of the little finger, if it is bent or if a person habitually curls this finger, the subject is bloody-minded. A V shaped gap between the middle fingers denotes some kind of rebelliousness.

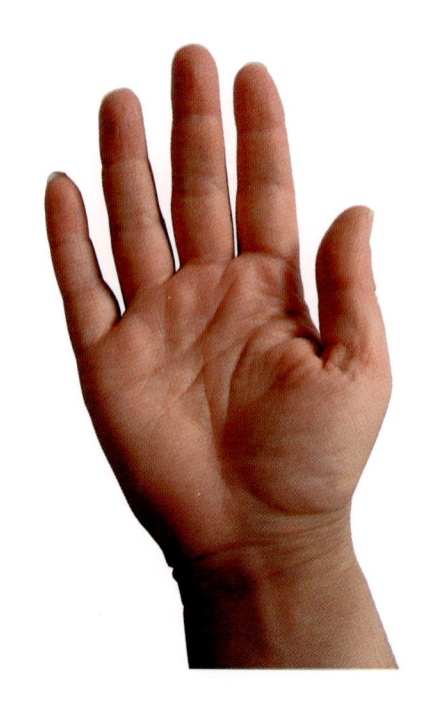

SECRETS ON DISPLAY

COLOUR

There is a lot that can be seen from the colour of the hands especially where health is concerned. Taking racial differences into account, hands that are a strange colour or that look wrong are sending out a danger signal. A flaring red patch indicates a short-term problem related to the area of the hand that it appears upon. I remember seeing a woman who had a patch that looked for all the world like inflammation in the area of her hand relating to brothers and sisters. When I asked if there was something wrong in her family, especially pertaining to her brothers or sisters, she said that her sister had recently given birth to a handicapped baby. Problems caused by others can also be seen in patches of redness on the backs of the hands and fingers. (See more on colour in the health section of this book.)

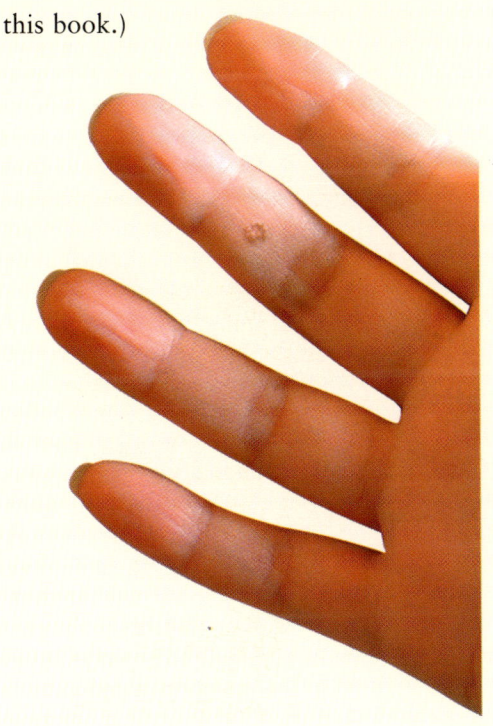

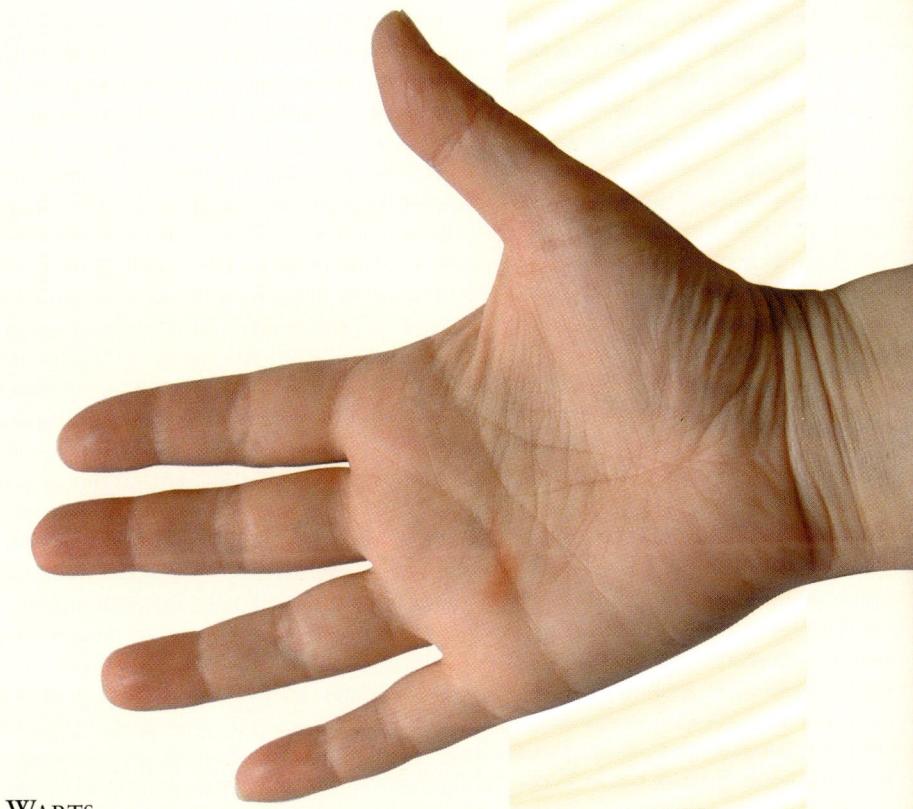

WARTS

Children frequently pick up wart viruses on their hands and feet and these mean nothing in terms of palmistry, but when an adult gets an isolated wart it is always worth taking into consideration. Note the finger or part of the hand this is on because it will imply a blockage in the smooth running of that aspect of the person's life. For example, a wart on the middle finger is a clear indication of financial insecurity while one on the ring finger indicates problems concerning property, the family or a love relationship. Some palmists say that a wart on the palmar side of the hand suggests that the blockage is self-imposed while one on the back of the hand is imposed by others.

Above: a flaring red patch indicates a short-term problem related to the area of the hand that it appears upon.

Left: a wart on the middle finger is a clear indication of financial insecurity

All Fingers and Thumbs

Below: it is worth using a ruler when assessing the true length of one finger against the next.

Fingers can be long, short, fat, thin, smooth or knotty. An artistic or a thoughtful person has longer fingers than an energetic go-getter, while broad fingers that are middle-sized and that have square tips suggest practicality. Knotty knuckles on the fingers belong to a deep thinker who does things at his own pace, while smooth fingers signify less thought but more and speedier action.

The length of the fingers in relation to each other is difficult for a beginner to ascertain because the way that these are set onto the hand must be taken into consideration. Fingers can be set onto the palm in a straight line, sloping from the index finger to the little finger or in an arc, so it is worth using a ruler when assessing the true length of one finger against the next. However, the setting itself has something to say. An arc setting suggests mental dexterity while the person with a straight setting can use his hands in a more practical way. Musical people sometimes have fingers that are set on a slope running downwards from the index finger to the little finger. Surprisingly, stumpy fingers can indicate an artistic or spiritual nature.

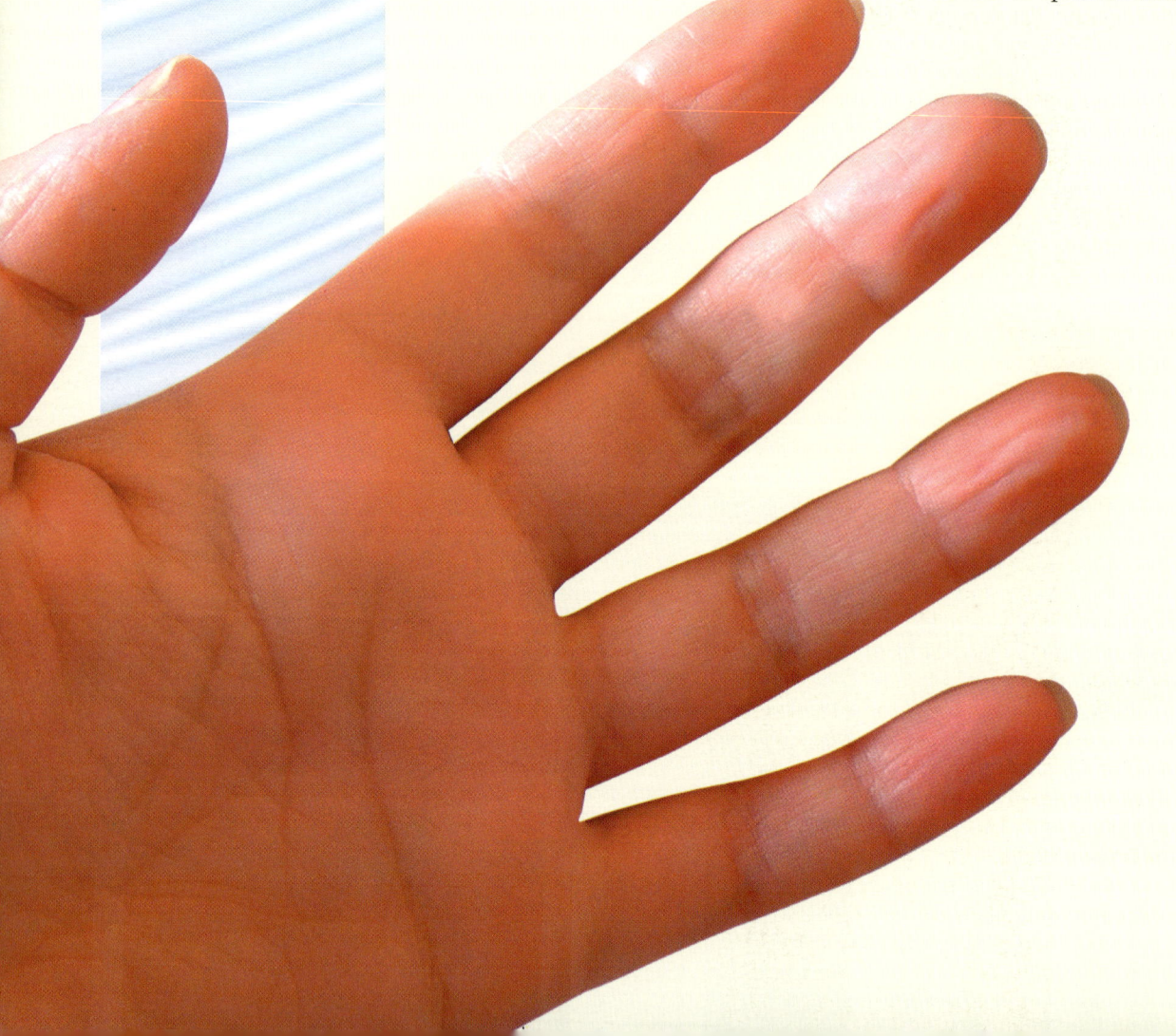

ALL FINGERS AND THUMBS

LENGTH OF THE FINGERS

Index (Jupiter) finger

The index (Jupiter) finger concerns leadership, the ego, self-confidence, bossiness and general attitude to life, also morals and idealism.

Long index (Jupiter) fingers shows leadership and a strong ego. Such people may have strong personal or religious beliefs or they may simply believe in themselves. They are attuned to their own needs or in getting a job done rather than spending time and energy on the needs and/or wishes of others. They believe that theirs (or their god's) ideas are the right ones. A person with short index fingers prefers to work as part of a team or on his own away from others. When the index finger bends towards the middle finger, the subject sacrifices time and energy for his family. He may also be wary of doing those things that will bring parental or spousal disapproval down on his head.

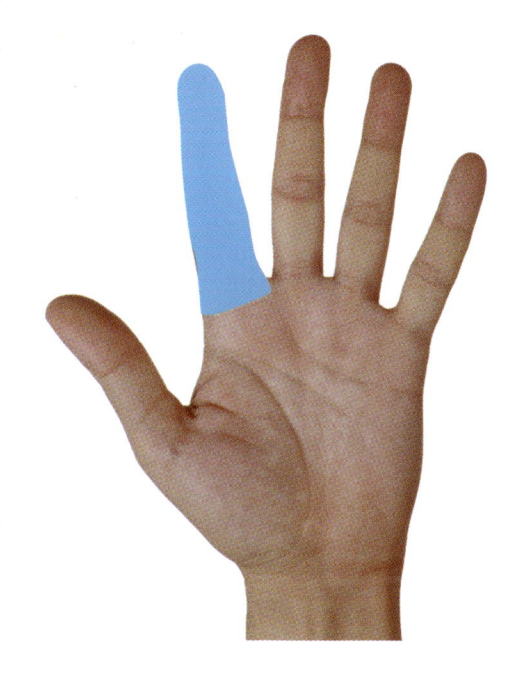

Left: the index (Jupiter) finger.

Below left: people with long index (Jupiter) fingers may have strong personal or religious beliefs.

ALL FINGERS AND THUMBS

Right: the middle (Saturn) finger.

Middle (Saturn) finger
The middle (Saturn) finger relates to a sense of responsibility, practicality and the kind of mind a person has, also to such things as an interest in science, philosophy and religion and the ability to save or spend money. If the middle finger is long, the subject has a talent for science and technical work; he may be somewhat dour and he could be a miser. If the fingertip and nail is square shaped, the subject is a good accountant or financier. If it is short, there is little sense of responsibility, the subject is a gambler or a waster and he will not see the need to provide money and comfort for anyone but himself. When it leans towards the ring finger, the subject needs to find work that he enjoys and, better yet, that gives him a creative outlet.

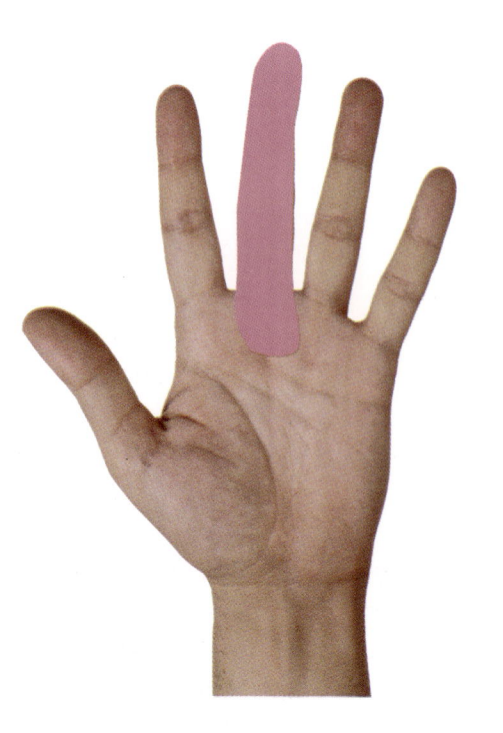

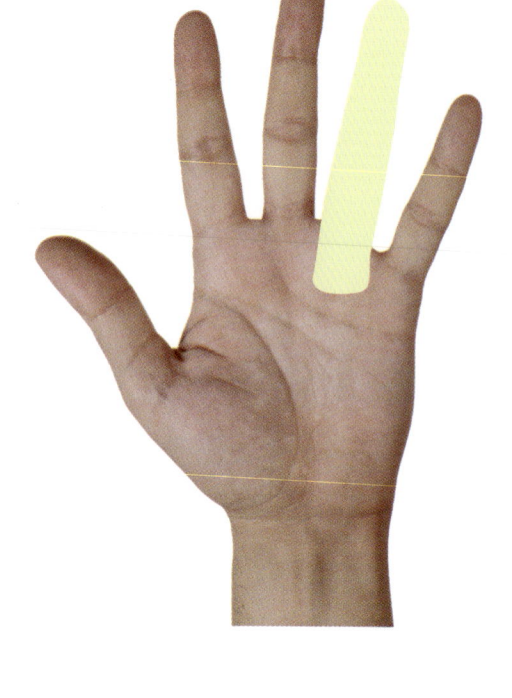

Ring (Apollo) finger
The ring (Apollo) finger concerns artistic or musical talent or appreciation, love and being part of a family.

It is often as long or even longer than the index finger which means that the subject is artistic, home loving and quick to sacrifice his own needs for those of his family. A short ring finger suggests little aesthetic or artistic appreciation and not much interest in home life either.

Right: the ring (Apollo) finger.

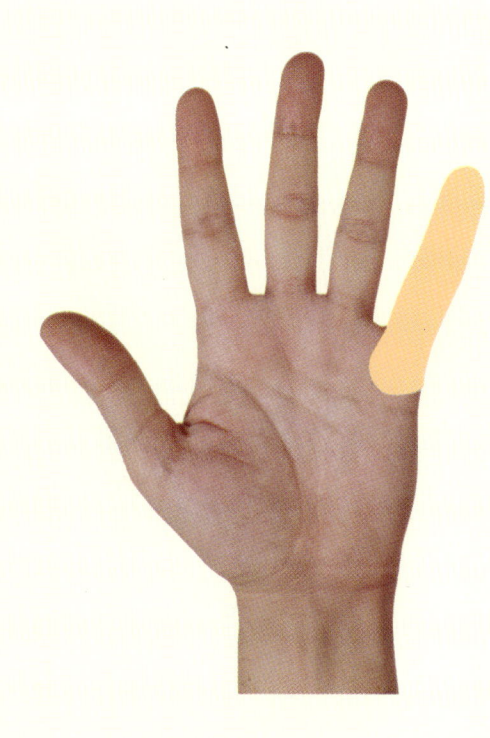

ALL FINGERS AND THUMBS

FINGERTIPS
Look at the shape of the fingertips and also the shape of the nails

1. Round
- *Friendly*
- *Adaptable*
- *If wide, lacking in vitality*

2. Narrow
- *Tense*
- *Babyish*
- *Charming*
- *Demanding*

3. Square
- *Scientific or mathematical mind*
- *Short, wide nails, witty and amusing*
- *Volatile*

4. Spatulate
- *Active*
- *Scientific*
- *Ambitious*
- *Sporty*

If the fingertips and nails are square, there is a talent for figure work or practical tasks. If rounded, the subject is sociable and creative, while pointed fingers can imply sensitivity and artistry but also stinginess. If the fingers and nails are a little like a spade at the end (spatulate), the person is very original and apt to paddle his own canoe. Whether this originality translates into success or a life spent fiddling around and getting nowhere depends upon other factors.

Little (Mercury) finger
The little (Mercury) finger concerns relating and communicating.

When the hand is closed, the tip of the little finger should reach the crease on the ring finger, but this depends upon the way the fingers are set on the hand. If the little finger is particularly long, the subject will be a good orator, politician, salesman or lecturer. If it is especially short, the subject will find it extremely difficult to communicate. Such a person could avoid love relationships and even do without sex altogether due to an inability to relate, because in palmistry sex is considered to be a form of communication.

1.

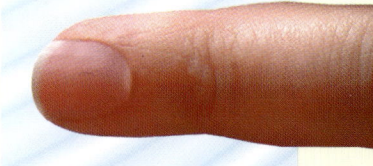

2.

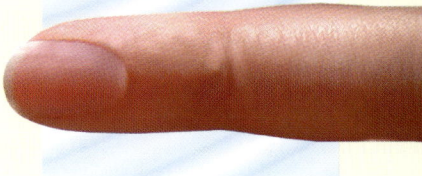

3.

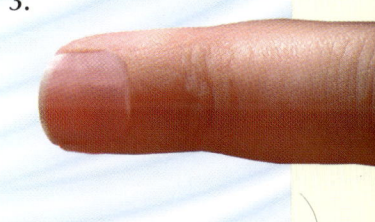

4.

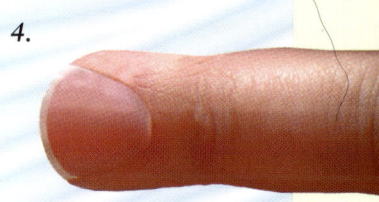

Above left: the little (Mercury) finger.

Fingerprints

The police use the same terminology for the fingerprints as hand readers do, but they don't necessarily impart the same meanings.

The only fingerprint patterns that are likely to turn up on every finger are the loop and the whorl. The loop is the most common print feature. Loops denote a normal personality who likes variety in life and who enjoys the company of others. Loops are either called "ulnar loops" or "radial loops".

Ulnar loops are by far the more common and these enter the finger from the percussion side of the hand. Radial loops can occur with some frequency on the index finger and very occasionally on the middle finger. On the index finger they indicate leadership qualities (and bossiness), and when on the middle finger, they denote a go-it-alone attitude to practical jobs such as do-it-yourself tasks or working as a self-employed electrician, plumber, builder and so on.

Loop
- *A team worker*
- *Adaptable*
- *Reasonable*

Whorl
- *Powerful personality*
- *Self-centred*
- *Success comes easily*

Arch
- *Tense*
- *Introvert*
- *Shy*

Double loop
- *Indecisive*
- *May be psychic if on Jupiter or thumb*
- *Can stand outside of self*

Peacock's Eye
- *Creative*
- *May be artist, craftsman, writer, teacher*

ALL FINGERS AND THUMBS

Whorls show independence, determination, a go-getting attitude and some selfishness when on the index finger, but whorls on all ten fingers either denote that the subject was born and lives in luxury or that he is lazy and disorganised. Arches signify a lack of confidence and a feeling that life is full of hard work. Arches are most frequently seen on the thumb and index fingers and occasionally on the middle fingers, but rarely on the ring or little fingers.

The peacock's eye denotes talent. It is most frequently seen on the ring finger, showing that the subject is a good home-maker and perhaps an artistic cook or gardener who enjoys arts and crafts. Much the same goes for the middle finger which often denotes a practical and artistic mix, such as someone who is a clever carpenter, builder or garden planner. When it is on the little finger, the subject is an excellent communicator, teacher or writer.

THE PHALANXES OF THE THUMB

The thumb is divided into two phalanxes (sometimes called phalanges).

The top joint determines the level of will power. If this is large and heavy-looking, the subject has a will of iron, and when thin the person is likely to be reasonable and co-operative. The second phalanx concerns the logical mind. When this is long or slim, the subject prefers to think before acting, but if it is short or thick he will act on instinct. A weak-looking ball on a weak-looking thumb signifies a lack of confidence and a lack of energy and determination – and possibly a weak mind.

When the base of the thumb is so flexible that the thumb can be easily worked back and forth against the hand, the subject can be influenced or put upon by others. An inflexible person has an inflexible thumb.

Below: the phalanxes of the thumb.

Top or first phalanx, determining will power

Second phalanx, relating to logic

Flexibility of the thumb base

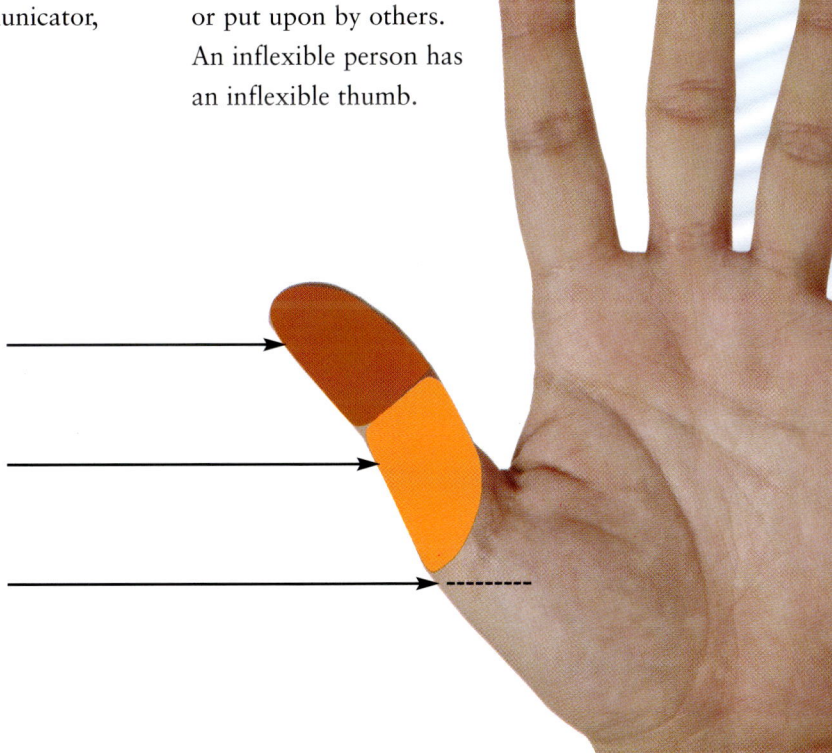

ALL FINGERS AND THUMBS

1. **Wedge-shaped**
• Keeps going until he gets what he wants
• Good lawyer or negotiator

2. **Rounded**
• Relates well to others
• Can exert authority when necessary

3. **Flat**
• Refined, gentle but lacks energy.
• Can get what he wants by nagging

4. **Spoke-shaved**
• Refined, pleasant, needs approval
• Gives way to others

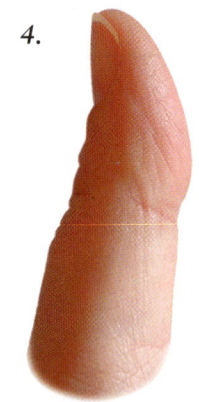

ALL FINGERS AND THUMBS

THE PHALANXES OF THE FINGERS

Each finger usually has three phalanxes. I say usually because very occasionally a little finger can have two or even four phalanxes.

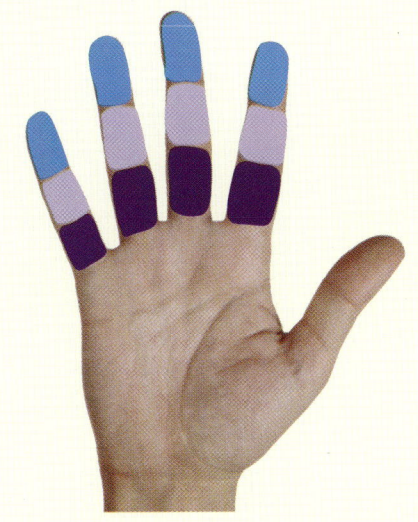

The top phalanxes refer to mental activity, the middle ones to action and the lower ones to the need for basic security. Therefore, a thinker will have long fingertip phalanxes and, if this subject also has creative talent, the pads on the fingers will appear to come to a point that palmists call droplets.

A person who puts thoughts into action will have a balance between the top and middle phalanxes. Short fingertip phalanxes and long or thick middle phalanxes indicate a person who acts without thinking very much first. A person who likes their creature comforts and who needs security will have long or perhaps rather fat lower phalanxes.

● *First (top) phalanx, mental activity.*

● *Second (middle) phalanx, action.*

● *Third (lower) phalanx, need for security.*

1. Coarse
- *Down to earth*

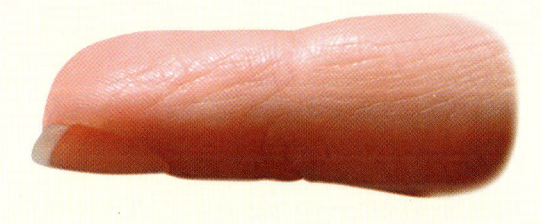

1.

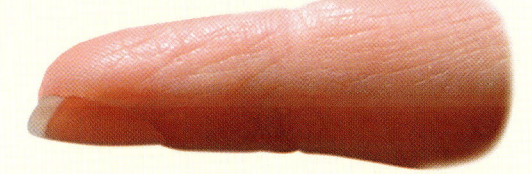

2. Tapered
- *Spiritual mind, but lacks stamina*

2.

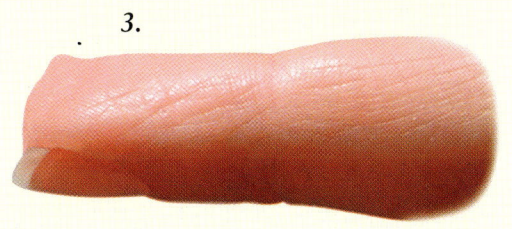

3. Droplet
- *Dexterity with hands*

3.

GETTING AROUND THE HAND

The different parts of the palm of a hand are traditionally called mounts, despite the fact that some of these look more like valleys.

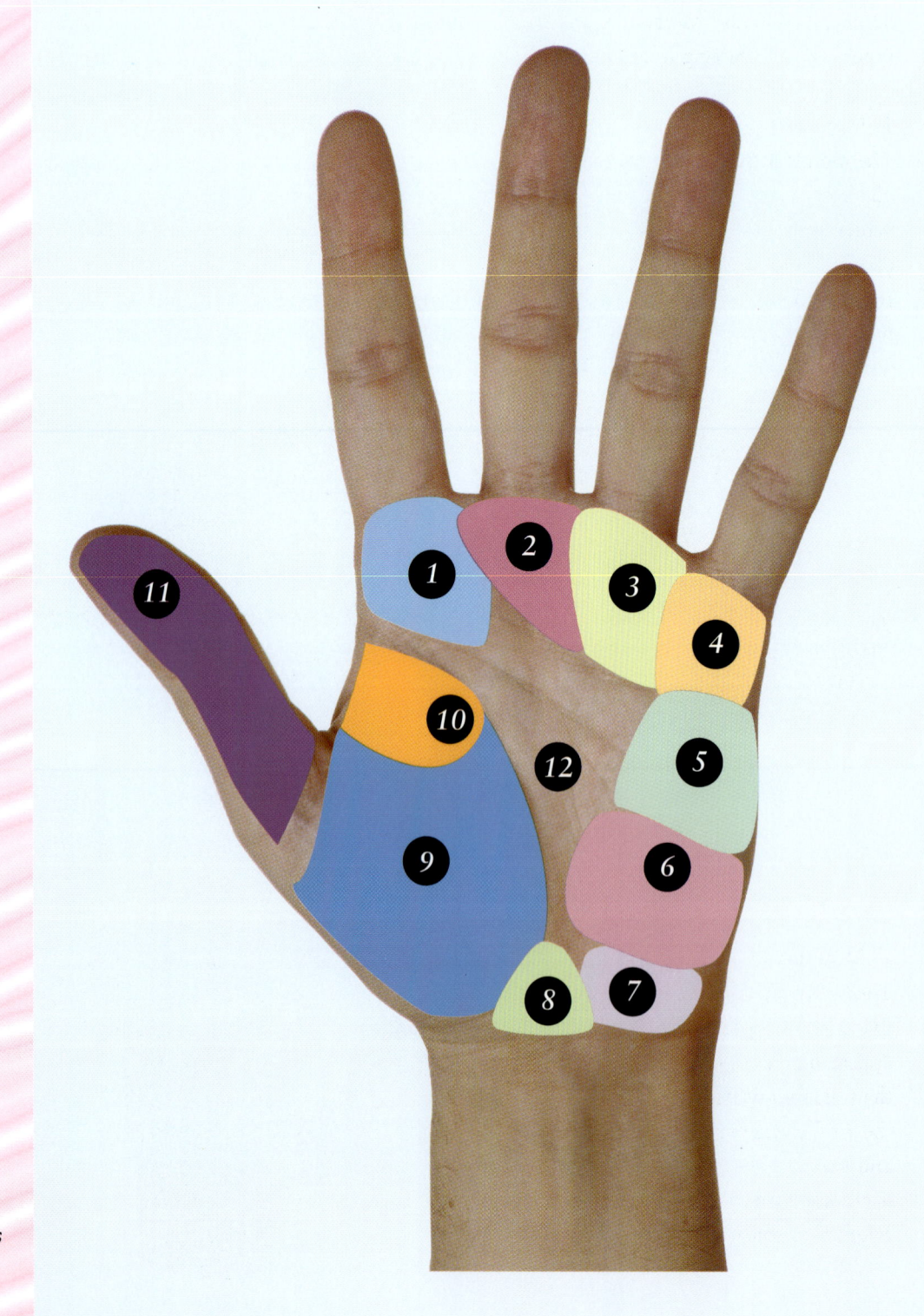

1. Jupiter
2. Saturn
3. Apollo
4. Mercury
5. Upper Mars
6. Luna
7. Pluto
8. Neptune
9. Venus
10. Lower Mars
11. The Thumb
12. Plain of Mars

GETTING AROUND THE HAND

The Mounts that Lie Beneath the Fingers

Although I have avoided calling the fingers by their ancient names of Jupiter, Saturn, Apollo and Mercury, there is no other way of referring to the mounts.

1. Mount of Jupiter

The mount of Jupiter relates to the ego, idealism, wisdom, success and achievement. If this is very prominent the ego is all too evident, but when it is flat the person lacks confidence. A moderate mount here suggests a nice balance.

2. Mount of Saturn

The Saturn area looks more like a valley than a mount and it is the lines that appear here that are more interesting than the mount itself. Having said that, if the area between the base of the fingers and the crease that is called the heart line is cramped (see page 48), the person might be a touch crabby and difficult to live with. There may be a loop formation on the pad under the place where the middle and ring fingers join the hand, which suggests that the person works hard, possibly in a creative job.

3. Mount of Apollo

The mount of Apollo, like the mount of Saturn, is often a valley and here, too, it is the lines that show up that are more interesting than the mount itself.

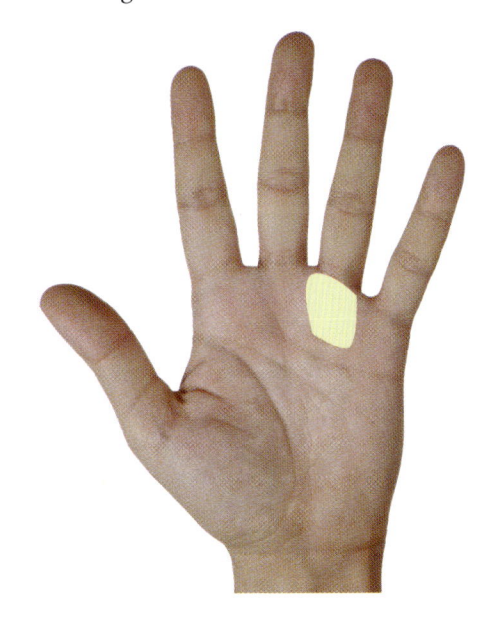

Left: the mount of Saturn.

Far left: the mount of Jupiter.

Below left: the mount of Apollo.

GETTING AROUND THE HAND

4. Mount of Mercury
The mount of Mercury is usually quite padded, and if it is also a fairly large or well developed, the subject is a good communicator and may be clever with computers and other technology.

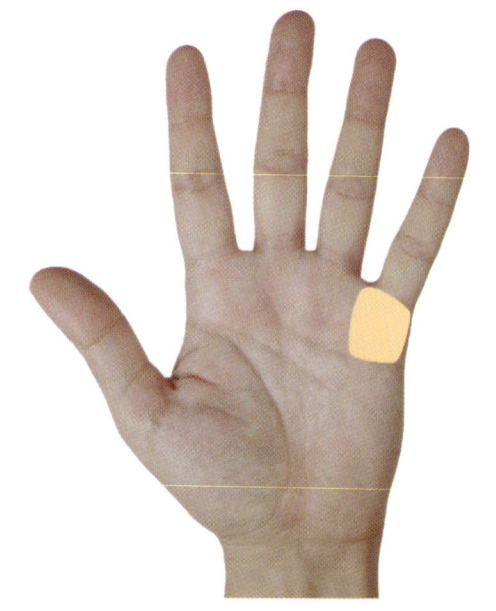

Right: the mount of Mercury.

Below: a person with a well-developed mount of Mercury may be clever with computers and other technology.

GETTING AROUND THE HAND

5. Mount of Venus

The mount of Venus is the large area that is bounded by the thumb on one side and the life line on the other.

The Venus mount is concerned with a love of luxury, the accumulation of possessions, possessiveness and zest for life and also love, sex and affection. A high mount of Venus shows a passion for life and a love of possessions. Music may feed the soul of this person or he may collect valuable and beautiful artifacts. Tradition tells us that a person with a full mount of Venus is sexy, and, while this is often true, this subject is also self-indulgent. Such a person is likely to travel and to accumulate a nice home and plenty of goodies. If the mount is high and full as well as large, the person is extremely charming when he wants to be, but can also be possessive, jealous, selfish, thoughtless, stingy, hurtful and unpleasant. However, this is just the person to hire for a tough sales job where closing the deal at any costs is the name of the game.

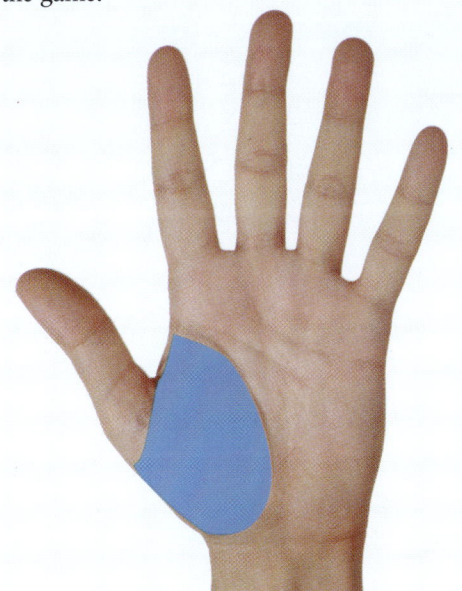

A flat mount of Venus belongs to someone who needs a quiet life and who probably prefers office work to challenges or adventure. He may find travelling or going into unknown situations terrifying, especially if the Venus area is cramped. If this area is wide, the subject will be quite big-hearted but if narrow could be difficult to live with. Those with small or narrow Venus areas don't hanker much after possessions, and they can live quite Spartan lives.

Above: the Venus mount is concerned with a love of luxury and the accumulation of possessions.

Left: the mount of Venus.

GETTING AROUND THE HAND

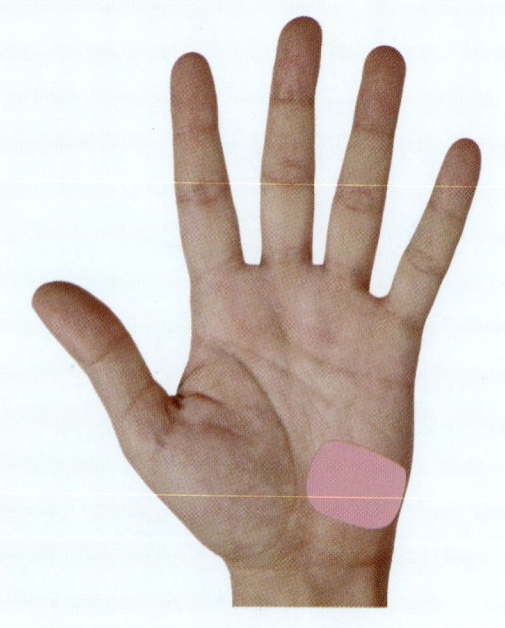

Right: the mount of Luna (the moon).

Far right: the mount of Upper Mars.

Below: upper Mars relates to fighting ability and emotional reactions.

THE MOUNTS OF MARS
Now things get a little complicated because the whole of the central area of the hand is devoted to Mars, but it is subdivided into upper Mars, lower Mars and the plain of Mars.

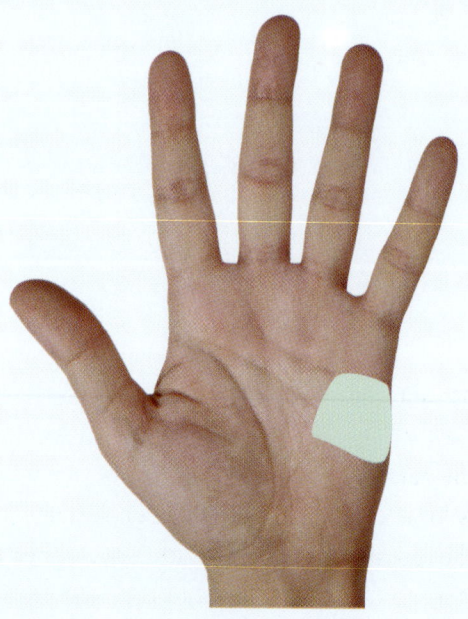

Mount of Luna
This area can be high or flat. It is concerned with travel and also with the imagination and, to some extent, psychic ability. A high mount, with the area that is now called Pluto dipping down towards the wrist suggests an adventurous personality who enjoys travelling and a change of scene. A creative or imaginative dreamer also has a large or high mount of Luna.

Mount of upper Mars
Upper Mars is located at the percussion edge of the hand and relates to fighting ability and emotional reactions. If this area is full, the person is unlikely to be surprised by much; he won't be intimidated by others and he may fight verbally or with his fists. The subject may choose to serve in the armed forces or fight for justice or moral reasons or he may pick fights for no reason at all. If this area is thin, the person is easily flabbergasted and he won't cope with bullies or stand up for himself, and he definitely wouldn't volunteer to join the army or stand on a picket line.

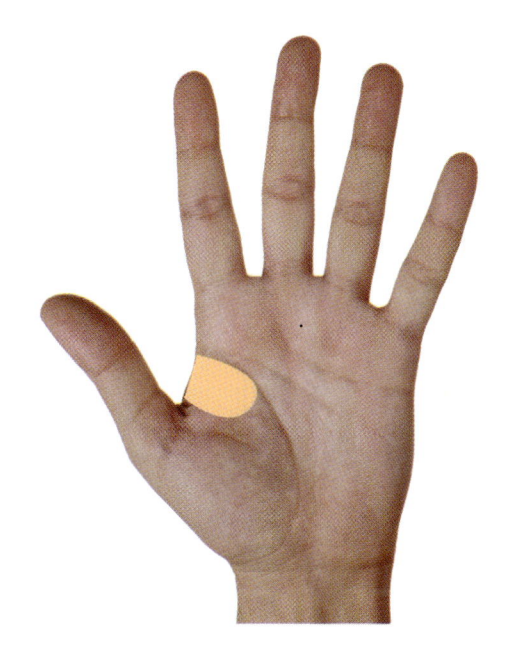

GETTING AROUND THE HAND

Mount of Neptune
This is the area just above the wrist and it represents a link between the conscious and unconscious mind and also the spiritual and the material world.

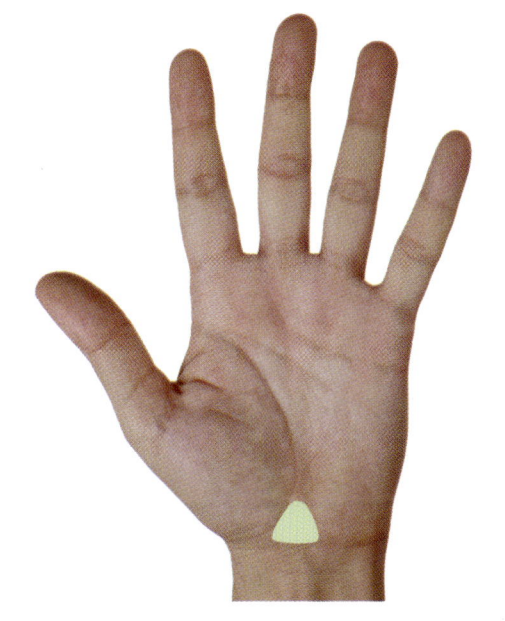

Mount of lower Mars
Lower Mars is often actually higher on the hand than upper Mars. Lower Mars is located on the hand and palm where the thumb opens away from the hand and it is inside the life line. Someone with prominent, large or "full" lower Mars mount can be counted on to do his duty. This subject probably enjoyed being part of a youth organisation such as the scouts or something similar when young. If this person was drafted into the forces for any reason, he would get a great deal out of the experience and he would put a great deal back into it. A flat or small area here belongs to an individual who sees no need to join pressure groups or to march around in a uniform.

A person who is purely materialist in outlook with no real connection to the world of dreams won't have much of a Neptune mount. A person who uses his imagination in a creative way and who is tuned into his inner consciousness will have a well-developed mount. Psychics, spiritual mediums, artists, psychologists, dream analysts, creative people and those who travel have well-developed Neptunes.

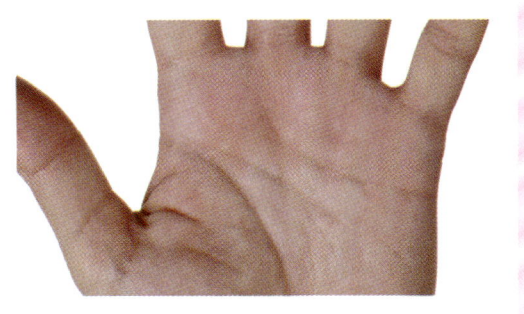

Plain of Mars
The plain of Mars is the area in the centre of the hand. It has no meaning of its own, but this is where many of the lines of the hand criss-cross.

Far left: the mount of lower Mars.

Left: the mount of Neptune.

Below left: the plain of Mars – the area in the centre of the hand.

GETTING AROUND THE HAND

ANGLES
It is worth talking about a couple of the angles on the hand.

Angle of rhythm
The joint where the thumb meets the hand is called the angle of rhythm, and if this is reasonably well developed the person has a sense of timing.

This sense of rhythm can be useful for sports and other active pastimes or for the kind of timing that a comedian or a rap artist needs, or for music or dancing.

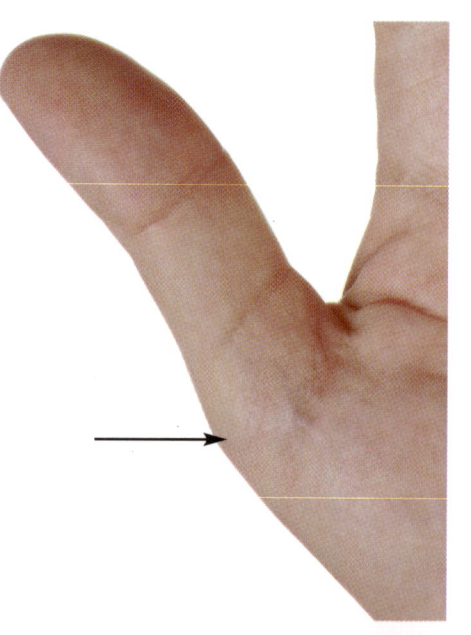

Right: the angle of rhythm.

Below: the sense of rhythm can be useful to a sports person.

GETTING AROUND THE HAND

Angle of music and melody
The angle at the very base of the hand where it meets the wrist on the thumb side shows a love of music and melody.

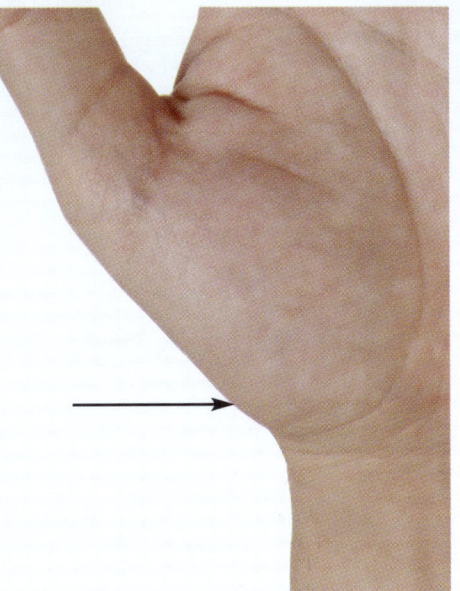

Above: *the angle of music shows a love of melody and music.*

Left: *the angle of music.*

What the Lines can Tell

Long Life and Good Health – or is it?

Most people think that a long life line indicates a long life – but this ain't necessarily so. A long, strong life line indicates strength and better recovery from a serious illness than a weak-looking one, but people can live long lives despite having short life lines. I once met a woman who had only a stump of life line on her left hand. She told me that she had been in a terrible accident as a child, but she had completely recovered from this after a longish spell in hospital. The other lines on her hand were normal, as was her right hand.

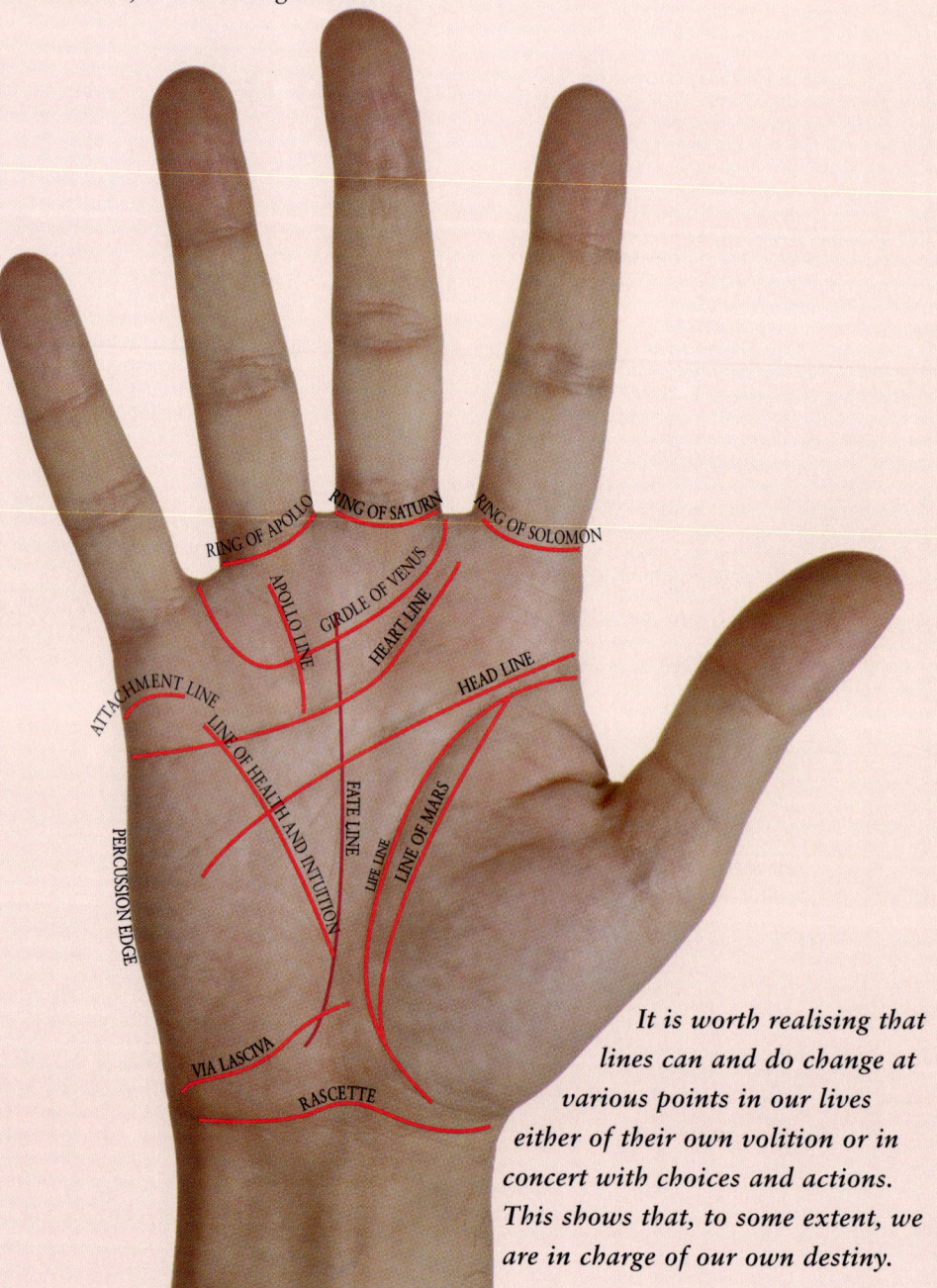

It is worth realising that lines can and do change at various points in our lives either of their own volition or in concert with choices and actions. This shows that, to some extent, we are in charge of our own destiny.

Right: the main lines on a palm.

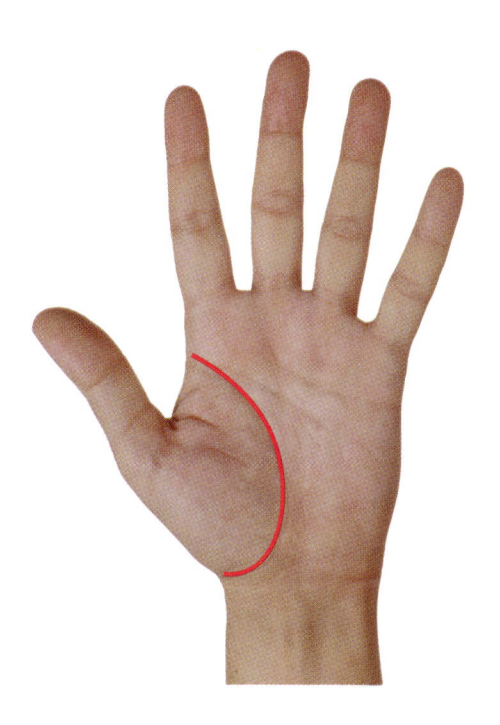

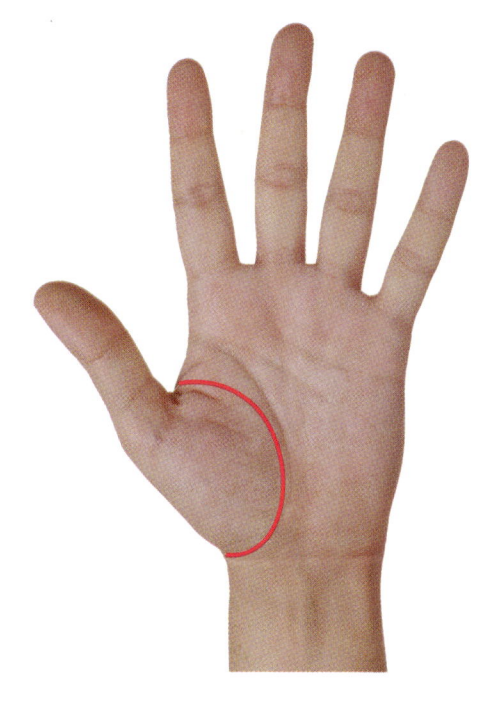

WHAT THE LINES CAN TELL

Far left: the life line starting high up.

Left: a life line creeping closely around the thumb.

Below: a good strong life line with few breaks indicates a person who prefers a job which involves using physical energy.

Life line
A strong life line that travels down the hand with very few breaks and little interference suggests good recuperative powers and it also signifies energy. Such a person prefers a job or lifestyle that involves using physical energy. He would dig the garden, do jobs around the home and work on his car and also enjoy active sports. If the life line also sweeps out into the hand he could be a restless traveller, a workaholic or someone who chases after a variety of sexual experiences. A strong life line also suggests a fairly straightforward life. The life line can start fairly high up almost on the mount of Jupiter, indicating an idealistic outlook, or at the side of the hand above the thumb, suggesting a more practical, physical and sensual approach.

Close life line
If the life line creeps closely around the thumb, the subject needs peace and a quiet well-ordered life.

WHAT THE LINES CAN TELL

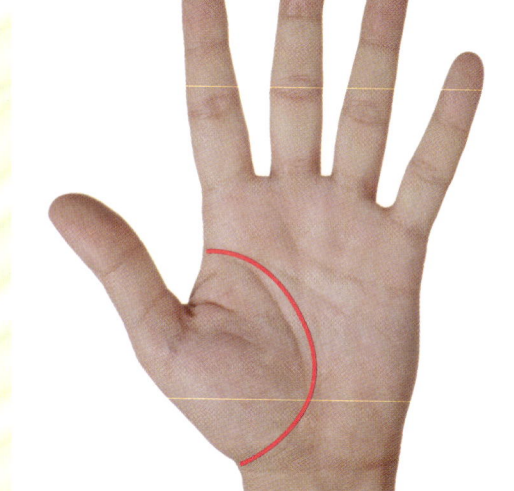

Right: a wide life line.

Far right: a life line with a fork.

Below: a wide life line indicates a career person.

A wide line and a wide fork
A life line that travels out into the palm of the hand suggests that the subject is more interested in a career or business than in sitting around at home. Sometimes the line forks at the end, showing the desire to for a career and travel in addition to a rich home and family life.

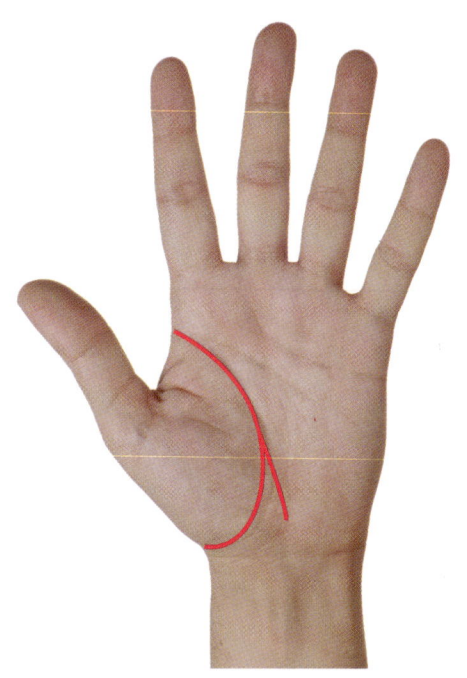

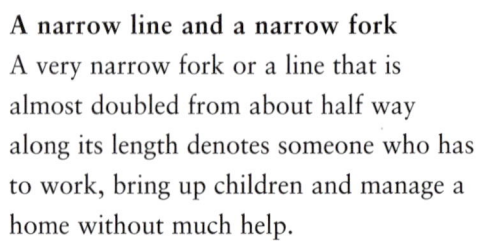

A narrow line and a narrow fork
A very narrow fork or a line that is almost doubled from about half way along its length denotes someone who has to work, bring up children and manage a home without much help.

WHAT THE LINES CAN TELL

Left: a broken life line indicate a changeable lifestyle.

Below left: a narrow double life line.

A broken life line

Sometimes the line breaks up and starts again a little later on. Old-time palmistry books used to put this down to sickness, accidents, disastrous loss or some other calamity, but modern palmists know that this shows a changeable lifestyle. Those who have a happy childhood, marry well, have a steady job, live in the same house for years and don't go anywhere don't have broken life lines.

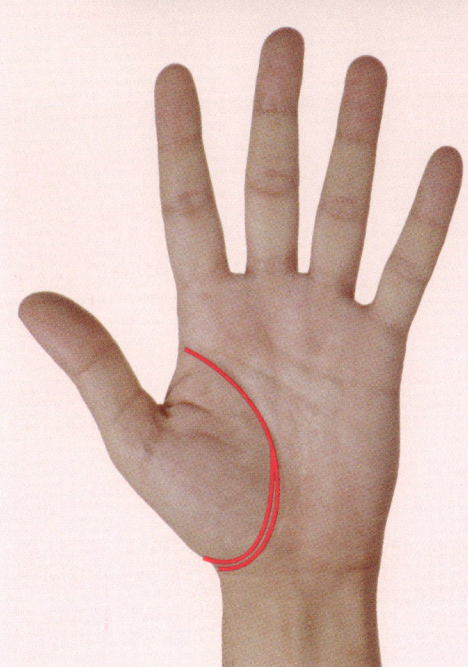

WHAT THE LINES CAN TELL

Broken line
A very common scenario is a life line that ends abruptly half way down the hand. A new piece of line then appears lower down, either further out into the palm or closer to the thumb. If you look closely, you will often be able to see a very fine line linking the old section to the new one. This indicates a sudden change of lifestyle that encourages the subject to put more into a career if the new piece of line is closer to the middle of the hand, or into a quieter and more homely lifestyle if it is closer to the thumb side of the hand. Such breaks and changes in lifestyle are often an indication of divorce or some other life-changing experience.

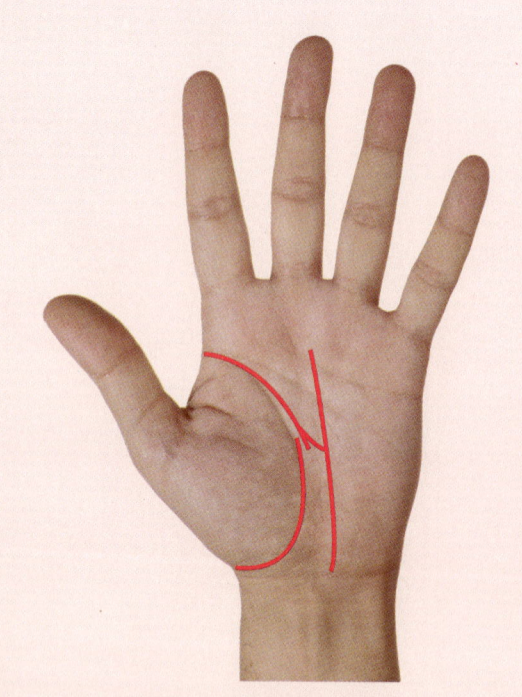

Right: a broken life line.

Below: a new section of line towards the bottom of the hand can indicate a new or better home.

New home line
A new section of line towards the bottom of the hand that curves towards the radial (thumb) side of the hand can indicate a new or better home later in life.

Bars, breaks, islands on life line
Breaks, bars, islands or other disturbances on the life line can indicate sickness, stress, worry, unsettlement or upheavals. It is worth checking out both hands for this because the trauma shows up more strongly on the minor hand than the major one. A long island on the life line shows a period of sacrifice or putting one's life on hold for a while, perhaps while taking time out to study or train for something new.

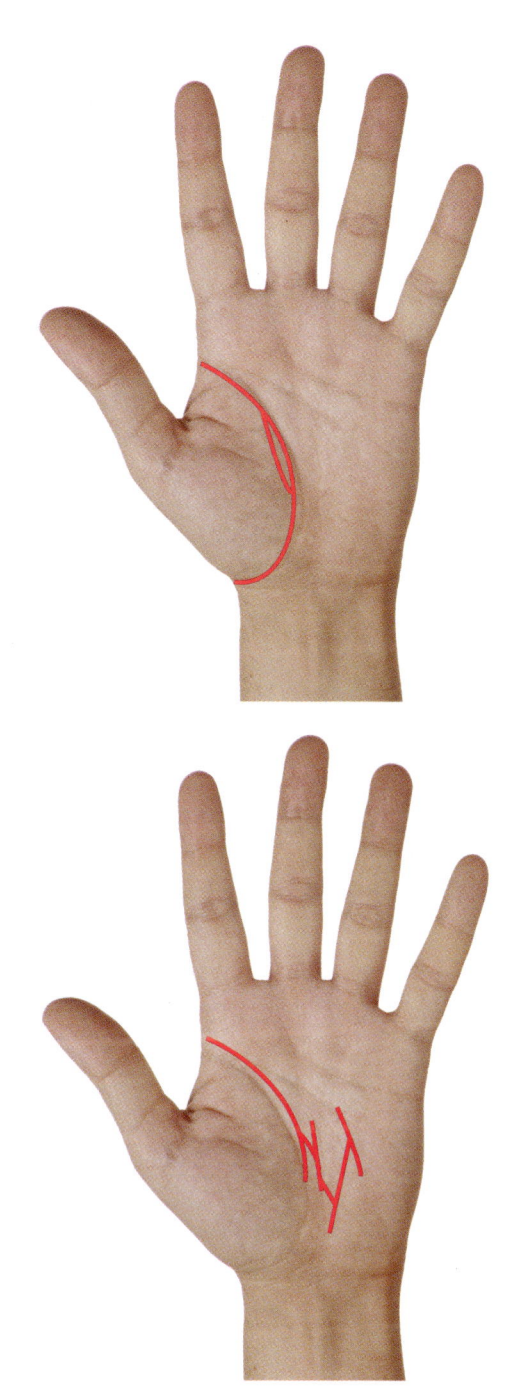

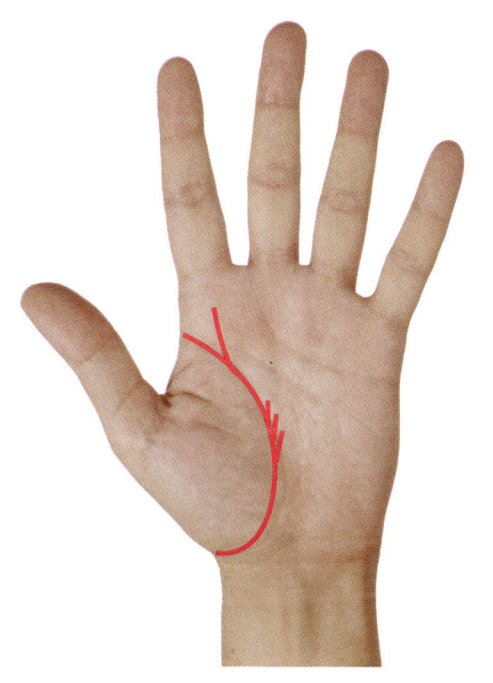

WHAT THE LINES CAN TELL

Left: lines rising from the life line.

Far left: an island on the life line.

Below left: rising and falling lines on the life line.

Shadow lines behind the life line signify that the person has good recuperative powers and spiritual protection of some kind. When asked, many people will say that they were close to their grandmother or some other family member and, despite the fact that this person is now dead, they feel their comforting presence during times of trouble.

Tiny pits on the life line indicate spinal problems. If the pits are close to the start of the line, these are neck problems and different parts of the spine are indicated as one moves down the line. If there are many pits and disturbances towards the lower end of the line, the person will have difficulty in walking.

Rising and falling lines
Lines that rise up from the life line show times of effort and also of success. Lines that fall down show things or people that are given up or that have run their course.

WHAT THE LINES CAN TELL

THE MIND, EDUCATION AND CAREER PROSPECTS

Head line
The head line starts on the thumb side of the hand and travels more or less across the hand. The starting point can vary a little but the ending point can vary a great deal. This line shows how the mind works and it gives information on education and the career.

Free head and life line
When the head and life lines are separated, the subject has supportive, protective and encouraging parents rather than harsh judges. He is more likely to stay in touch with his family and even to take his time about leaving the parental home. He has reasonable confidence and self-esteem and is able to make independent decisions and not beg for the approval of others.

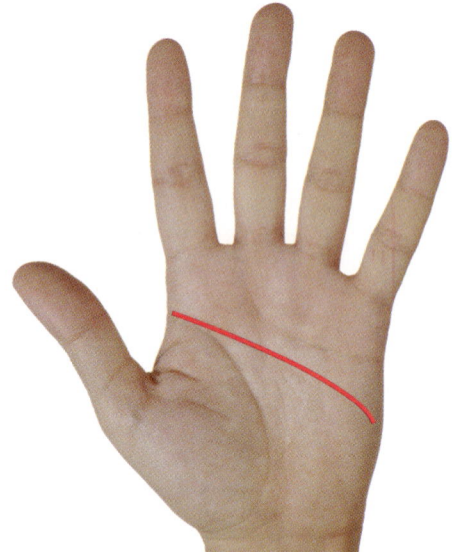

Right: the head line.

Far right: a free head line.

Below right: a tied head line.

Tied head and life line
Old-time palmists suggested that a tied head and life line indicated someone who didn't leave home or untie the apron strings until relatively late. In fact, this may be the exact opposite of what happens, because the person feels so dominated by his parents that he may leave home extremely early in order to free himself from their criticism and harmful behaviour. He is cautious and he lacks confidence, self-worth or self-esteem.

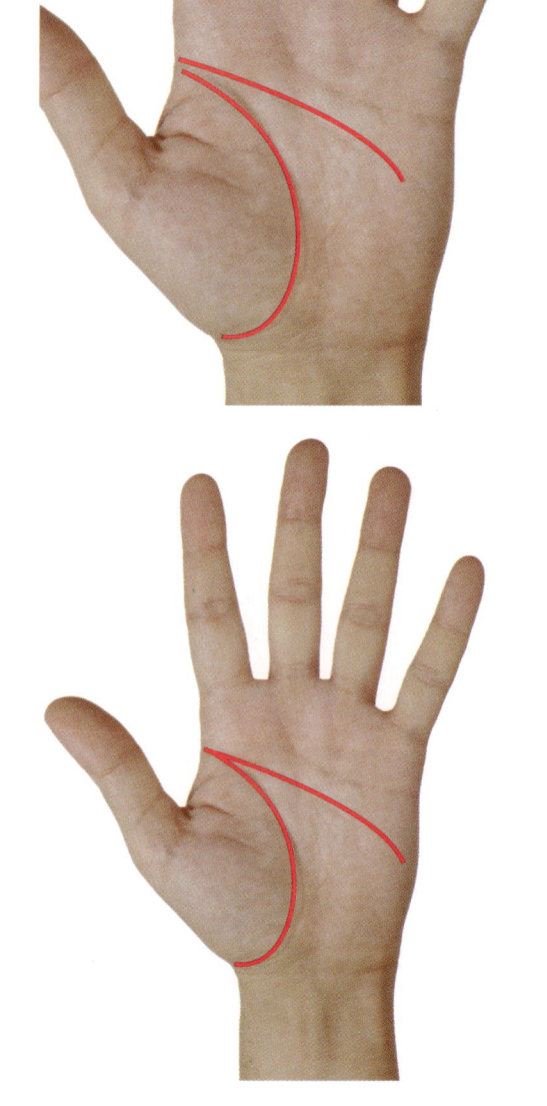

WHAT THE LINES CAN TELL

Left: the head line tells a palmist much about the ability and readiness of the subject to leave home.

WHAT THE LINES CAN TELL

Right: a cat's cradle pattern between the head and life lines.

Below right: a straight head line shows business sense and success.

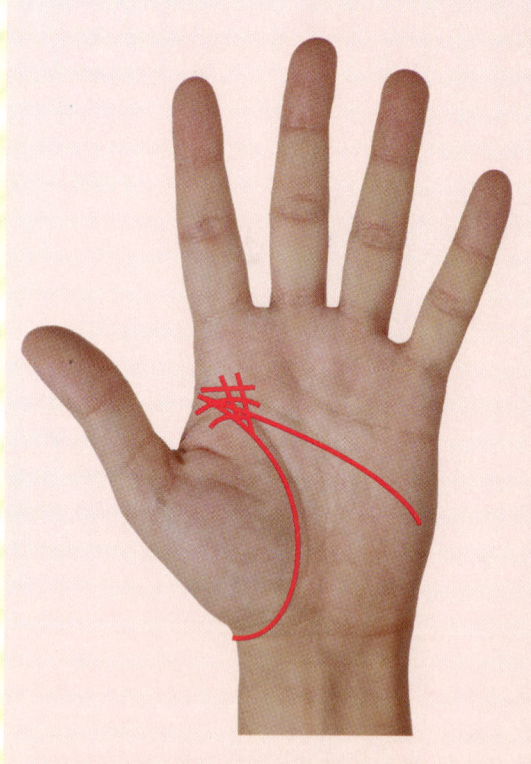

Cat's cradle
If there is a "cat's cradle" pattern between the head and life line where they part, the chances are that the person didn't like school very much – or, conversely, loved school and saw it as an escape from a difficult home life.

Curved or straight head line
A straight head line shows business sense and success. An upward flick or curve or a line flicking or curving up from the head line show business or career success. Someone with a straight head line that runs across the hand from side to side can cope with maths, computers and so forth. A sloping head line shows a more imaginative personality, perhaps being a "people person" rather than a lover of machines or methods.

WHAT THE LINES CAN TELL

Long or short head line
A long line suggests a person who never stops learning throughout life and who has many interests, while a short line shows a specialist who knows a great deal about one or two subjects but who doesn't have much breadth of vision.

Straight line with sudden dip
A line that travels across the hand and then suddenly dips denotes a person with an uncertain temper who can break out into sarcasm, rages or other unlovely behaviour.

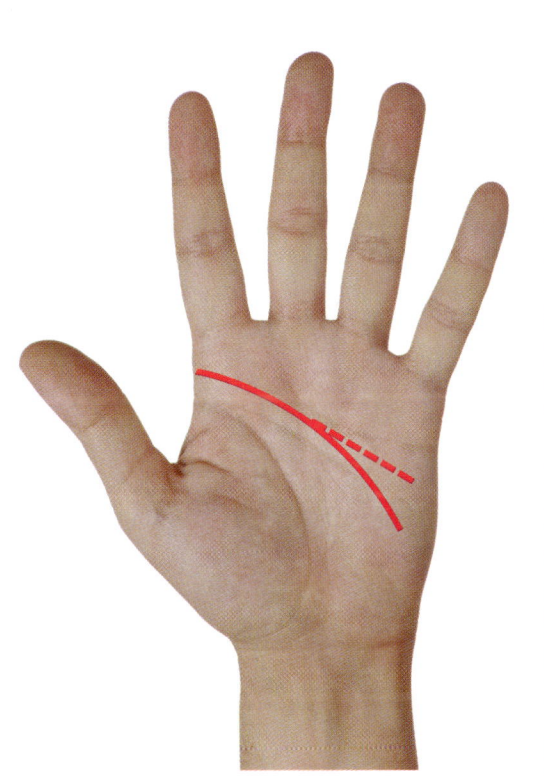

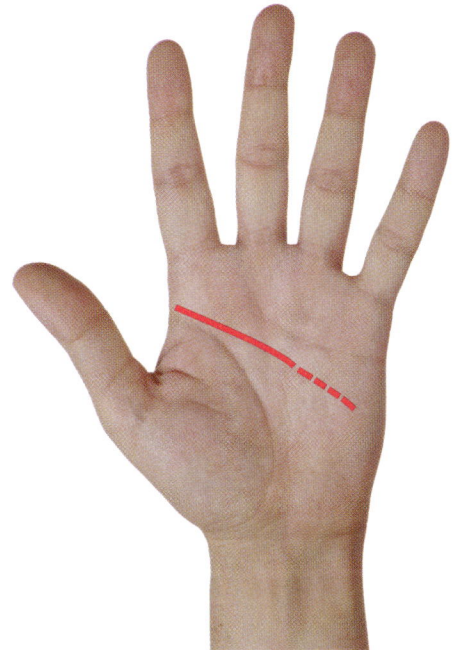

Left: a long or short headline tells a reader whether the subject is a specialist in one area or has many interests.

Below left: a straight line with a sudden dip.

Below: a long line also indicates that the subject never stops learning throughout life.

Right: *a wavy head line.*

Far right: *forks on the head line.*

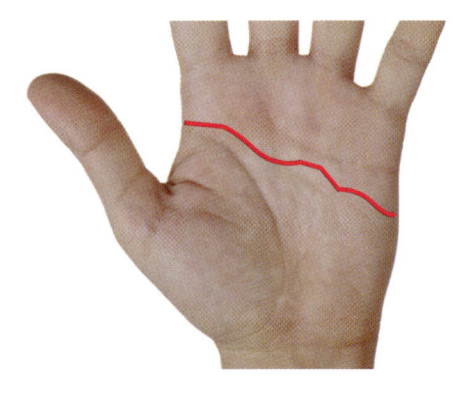

WHAT THE LINES CAN TELL

Wavy head line
A wavy head line signifies ups and downs in career or business matters.

Double head line
Forks, breaks, rising and falling lines are very common. A truly double head line with two distinct starting and ending points is very rare indeed, and it signifies that something is radically wrong with the person's brain. Much the same goes for a large and distinctive island which splits the line in two and then joins it again further along.

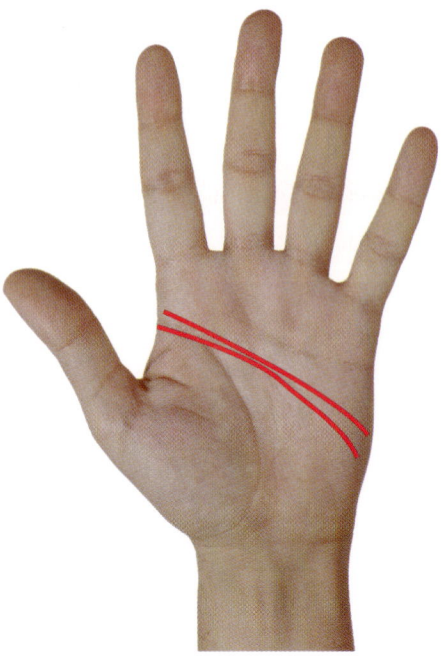

Forks on the head line
Forks are very common and they imply versatility. Deep forks on both hands can suggest that the person is too versatile to achieve anything; indeed this person may start many things and never get around to finishing any of them. Smaller forks denote communications ability and sometimes a talent for writing.

Chained head line
A chained head line can be an indicator of dementia in later life or just muddled thinking. Smaller chains indicate migraine or problems with sight or hearing.

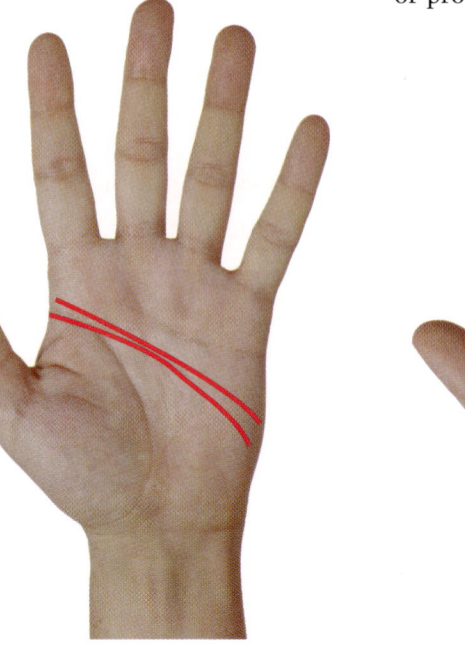

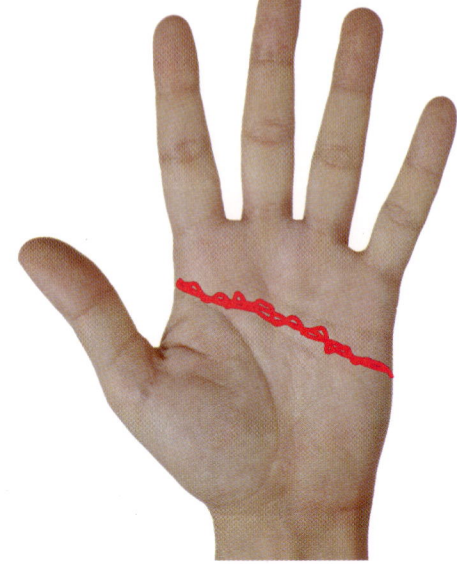

Right: *a double head line.*

Far right: *a chained head line.*

WHAT THE LINES CAN TELL

Left: small forks on the head line can indicate a talent for writing.

WHAT THE LINES CAN TELL

Branched head line
Branches that rise up from the head line denote achievements and success while those that branch down show things that have been abandoned either because they didn't work out or because they have run their course. Strong upward branches show a great deal of effort being put into something that leads to success. A branch that becomes a fork often means that the subject has two jobs or two distinct interests.

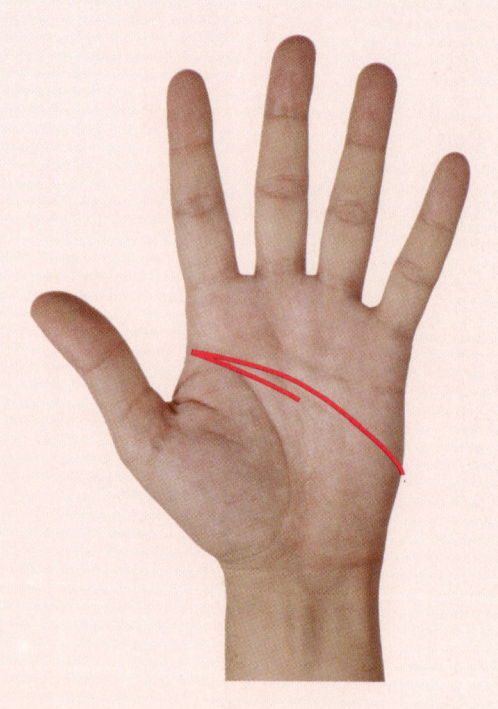

Right: a branched head line.

Far right: a small secondary head line.

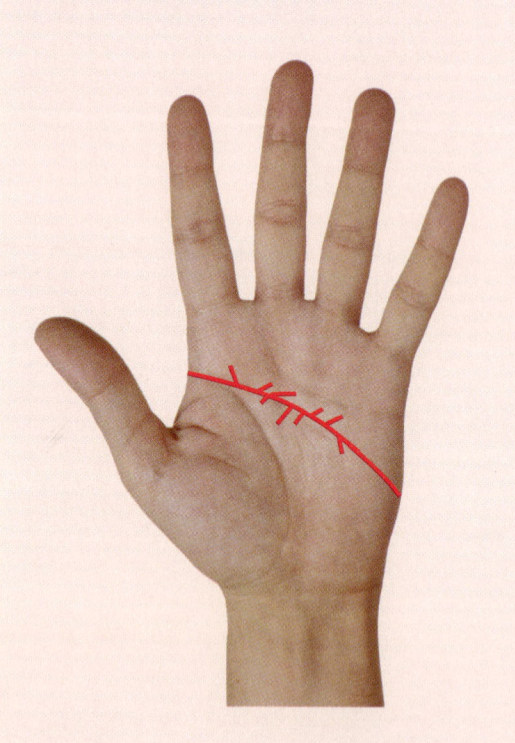

Small secondary head lines
Sometimes there is a small secondary head line that pops out from the life line and I have discovered this to indicate a secondary or parallel career in a totally different line of work from the main one. If this extra line is straight, the secondary interest is a scientific one; if curved, it is artistic or musical.

Too many forks and branches can show dissipation of energy, too many activities or perhaps too many demands being made on the person. Extra forks and lines will wither away if the subject changes his attitude or puts his foot down.

WHAT THE LINES CAN TELL

Left: branches that rise from the head line indicate achievements and success.

WHAT THE LINES CAN TELL

Islands on the head line
Islands on the head line signify periods of confusion at school or college, at work or in other spheres of life. These subjects often go through a period of feeling trapped at some point in their lives, either by a period of illness or by being in a dead-end job or for some other reason. An island that is almost diamond shaped can show a period of actual imprisonment.

Breaks, bars, starts and stops and lines that wander about and start again all indicate changes in direction, changes in aims and ambitions and changes of career. A really nasty break can indicate a head injury, sudden loss of sight, the onset of deafness or even trouble with one's teeth.

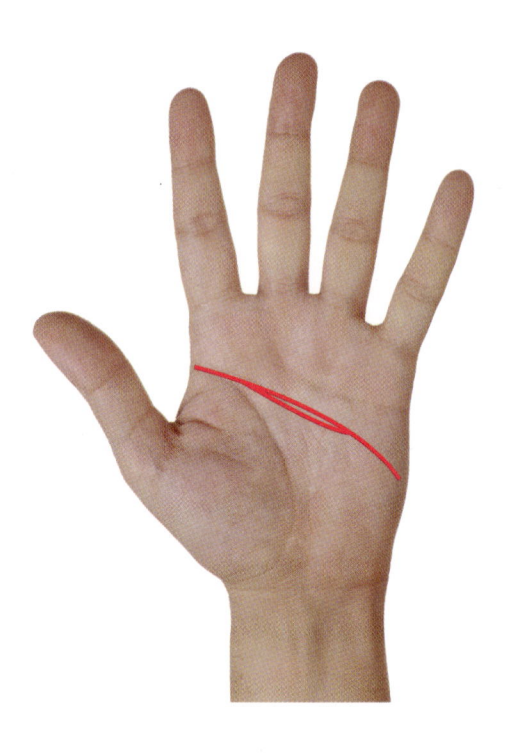

Right: islands on the head line can reflect a period in which the subject feels they are in a dead-end job.

WHAT THE LINES CAN TELL

Disturbances on the lines and what they look like   *What they mean*

Tassels — Usually at the end of a line: illness, weakness, senility.

Dots or pits — Illness. These come and go.
Chains — Confusion, lack of self-esteem. A troubled patch to live through.

Islands — Always important: trouble, shock, loss, sacrifice, hardship, unhappiness. If long, a refusal to face reality. If short, a short sharp shock.

Discoloration — Blotchy, discoloured patches or shiny, red, mottled patches denote illness.

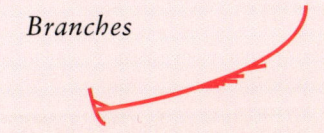

Branches — Upward branches on lines, denote improving circumstances, downward ones denote giving something up. Falling branches on the heart line denote a flirt.

Left: an island on the head line that is almost diamond-shaped can show a period of actual imprisonment.

WHAT THE LINES CAN TELL

WHAT WE NEED IS LOVE

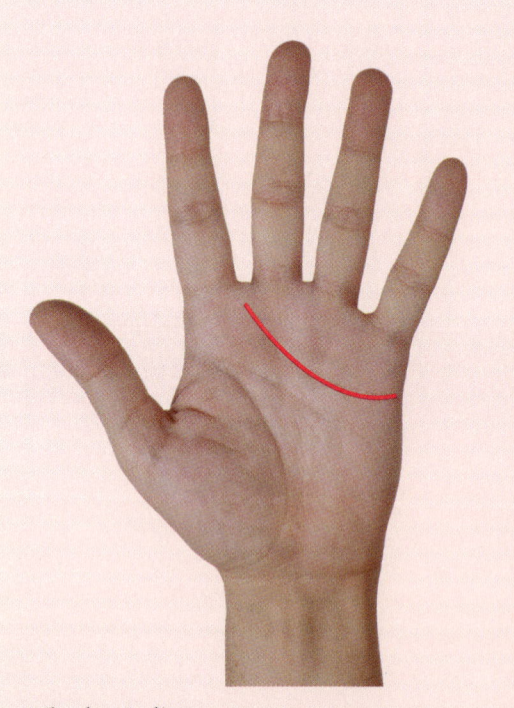

Right: the heart line.

Far right: a deep curved heart line indicating that the subject's feelings run very deeply.

The heart line
It would be really useful if the heart line tracked the progress of relationships and told us who we were going to meet, fall in love with and stay with – or leave. Unfortunately it doesn't! The heart line gives some information on these matters, but it tells us far more about *how* we love, in addition to some important health matters. Heart lines can be straight, curved, long, short and set high or low on the hand. They can be complete or broken.

Deep curved heart line
A deep heart line that leaves plenty of space between itself and the fingers shows that the person's feelings run deeply. If the heart line curves upwards towards the fingers, it shows a capacity for romantic love. This subject doesn't measure the object of his desires by anything but his own feelings. However, this person may expect too much of others or be somewhat intolerant and demanding.

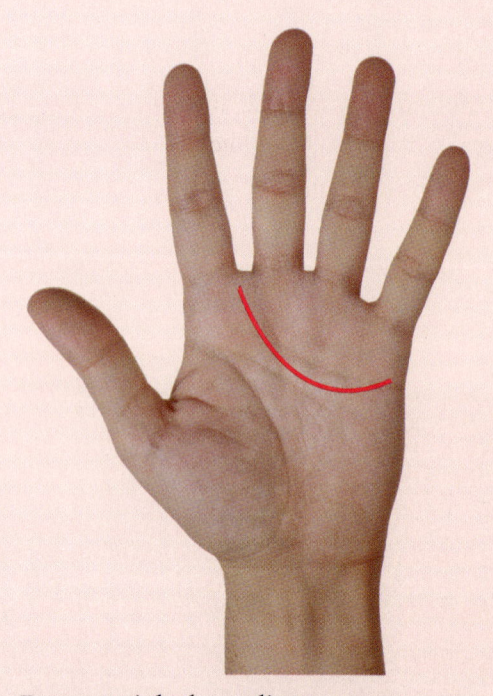

Deep straight heart line
If the line is deep and straight, the person will choose a life partner because they come from a particular kind of background which he considers to be "suitable". This means that issues such as race, religion, culture, education, family background, career, money and even the way a person dresses or speaks are important factors in this subject's choice of life partner.

Such a person can have a fling with an unsuitable person, but he won't want to take them home to mother!

WHAT THE LINES CAN TELL

It is also very interesting to see how each of these types copes with the break-up of a relationship. The curved heart line subject weeps, wails, talks about his hurt and then drinks, smokes and does foolish things – and then gets over it completely. The straight heart line subject broods, hates, never forgives or forgets. He may move on to further relationships quickly or he may wait before becoming involved with someone new, but he never really trusts again and he probably punishes the next partner for the supposed sins of the previous one.

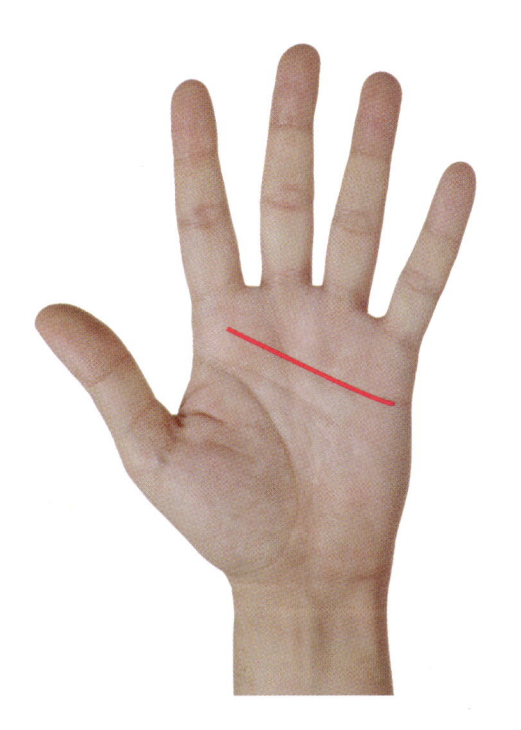

Left: a straight heart line.

Below: if the heart line curves upwards towards the fingers, it shows a capacity for romantic love.

WHAT THE LINES CAN TELL

Shallow short heart line
A shallow heart line suggests less ability to love. Sometimes this person wants to love and be loved but never quite manages to pull this off. One case that palmist, Malcolm Wright, quotes is of a women with a short, shallow heart line who had been married three times and who agreed that she really didn't know what love was!

Broken heart line
A heart line that has one break indicates disappointment or even a broken heart. Life goes on, though, and there is no reason why this subject should not find love again later on.

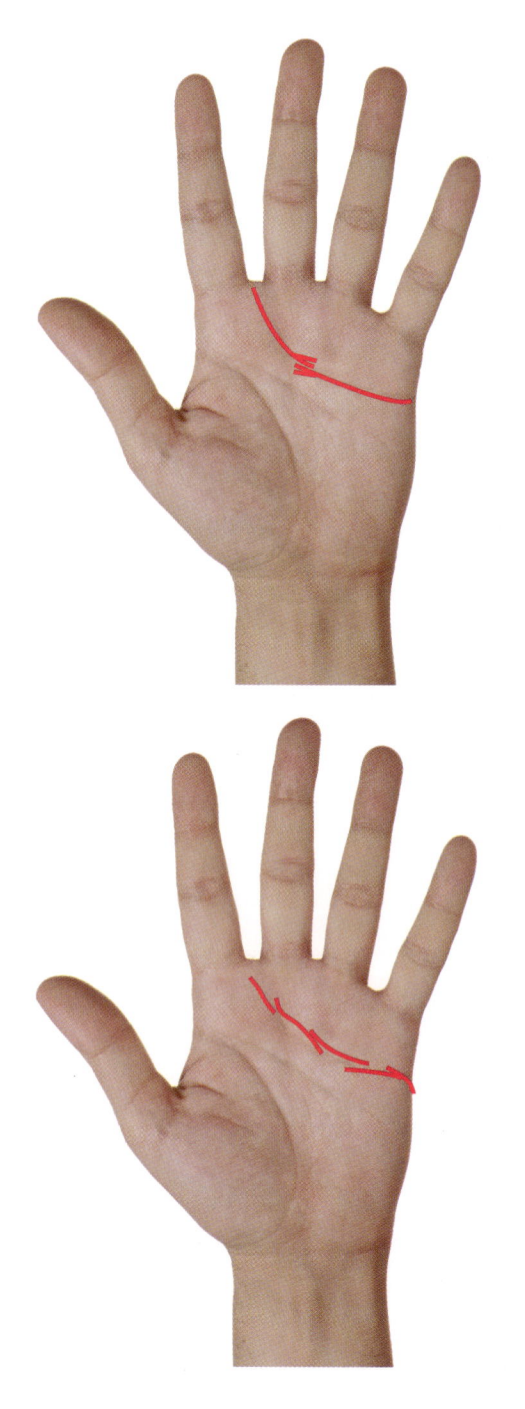

Right: a shallow short heart line.

Far right: a broken heart line indicating disappointment.

Below right: a fragmented heart line.

Fragmented heart line
A fragmented heart line is similar. Sometimes the subject is a loner. Sometimes a person is let down or disappointed early in life and then spends years pining over the idealised lost lover. To such a person, dreams are safer than reality. This person makes good friends and that may be enough.

WHAT THE LINES CAN TELL

Small break on curve of the heart line
If the heart line has a small break under the middle finger where it begins to turn upwards, the subject may never find love and sex in the same shop, so to speak!

Islands on the heart line
An island on the heart line means that the subject has or will have a shock due to a relationship coming to a sudden and unexpected end.

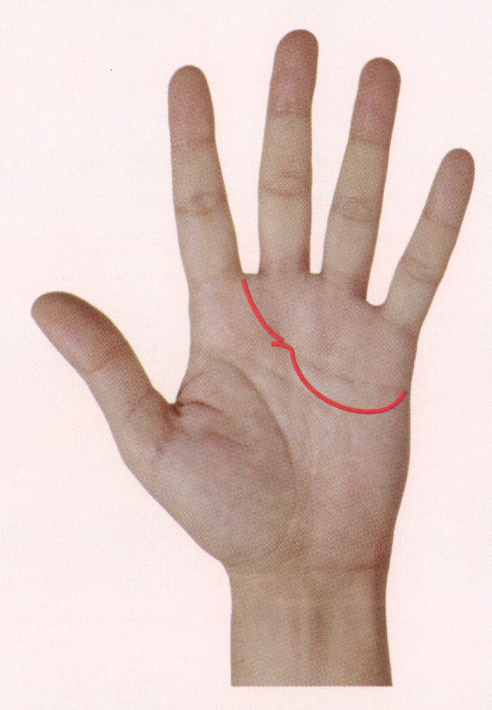

Left: a break on the curve of the heart line.

Far left: an island on the heart line.

Below: a break on the curve of a heart line suggests that the subject may never find love and sex in the same place.

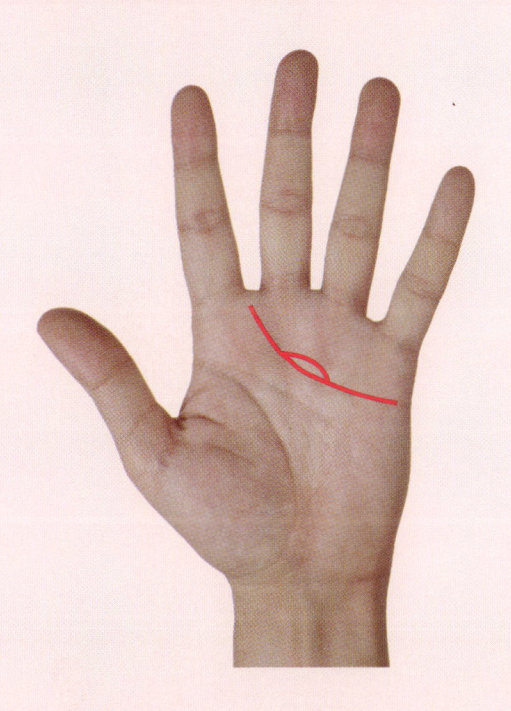

Many heart lines show forks or trailing lines where they curve. This indicates friendships as well as love. If there is one strong line that parts from the heart line and is attached to the beginning of the life line or head line, there may be something unpleasant in the person's childhood – possibly some kind of abuse. Check the way the thumb is held and see if the person holds it close to his palm.

WHAT THE LINES CAN TELL

Health on the heart line

Messy start to heart line
A spiky, tasselled or islanded start to the heart line indicates problems with the myocardium or arteries (check the colour of the nails and fingers). If you push a person's fingers back and find blue pits along the line, there will be lung damage.

If there is some kind of messy area where the heart line starts to curve upwards (if it does curve upwards), breast or chest trouble is indicated. This may or may not be due to cancer, because fibroids and cysts also show up here.

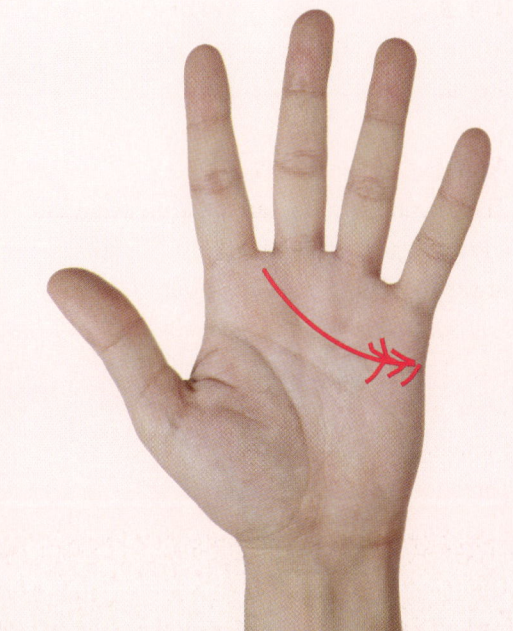

Right: a messy beginning to the heart line.

Below right: an islanded start to the heart line.

Below: blue pits along the heart line indicate lung damage.

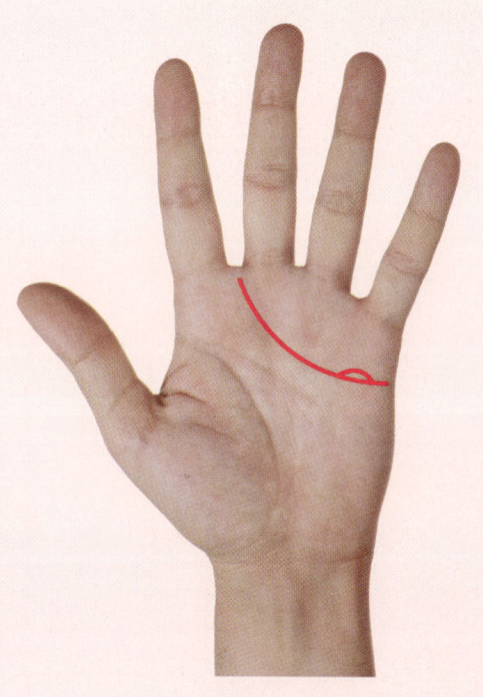

LOVE, PARTNERSHIP AND FAMILY

Marriage certificates are not shown on a hand, but feelings about those whom we share our lives with or those whom we give our hearts to are shown on the hand. Along with the heart line, the main area of interest for matters of love and partnership are the attachment lines, but there are other indications – as we will soon see.

ATTACHMENT LINES

The attachment lines are little creases that enter the palm from the percussion edge of the hand in the area between the bottom of the little finger and the heart line. There is some confusion because some old-time palmistry books consider these lines to show how many children a person will have.

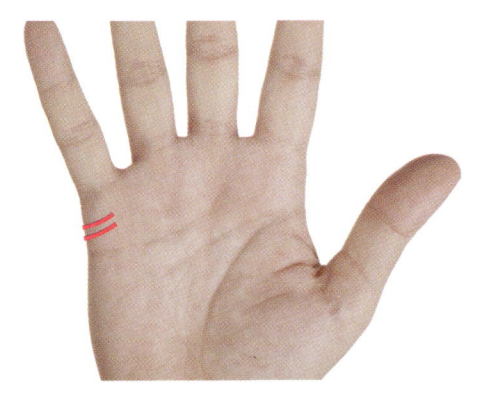

Left: attachment lines.

Below: marriage is not necessarily shown on the hand but the people we share our hearts with are.

LOVE, PARTNERSHIP AND FAMILY

How Many Relationships?

One attachment line
One strong attachment line can mean one long marriage-type relationship, but it can also show that the subject wants one long marriage in an ideal world. If a relationship fails, he will try to find another one that works better.

Two attachment lines
Two attachment lines suggest that the person will question relationships and if he thinks they don't come up to expectations, he will consider moving on. In this case, more than one marriage-type relationship is a strong possibility.

Multiple attachment lines
When there are more than one or two lines, the chances are that some lines are strong and some are faint. In this case, it is best to concentrate on the strong lines. If there are a number of lines and none of them stands out much, the person is still looking around and is not ready to settle down. The chances are that at a later date, some lines will fade out and one or two strong ones will emerge.

Disturbances on attachment lines
There will be no real relationship problems if the attachment line is clean and clear, but any disturbance to a main attachment line points to trouble. For example, a line that has an island on it denotes that the partner will be sick or troublesome at some point.

When the line forks or frays at the end, the marriage or relationship is already in difficulties and a split up may be on the cards. If a deletion line crosses the line or the forked or frayed part of the line, or even if it is very close to it, the relationship is unlikely to survive.

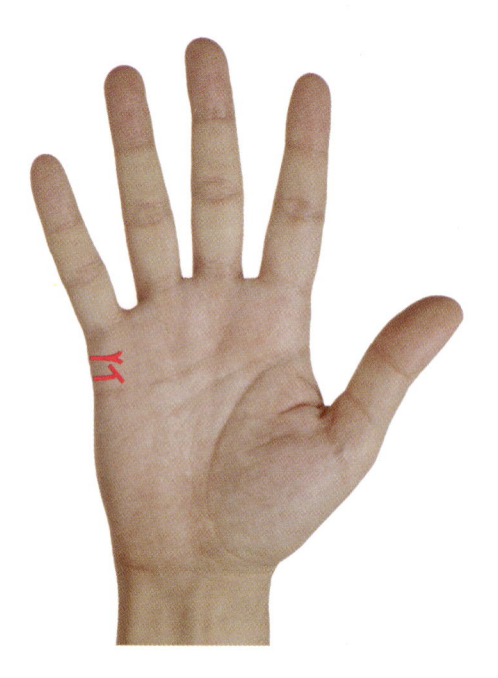

Right: a fork on one attachment line and a deletion line crossing the lower one.

Below right: an island on an attachment line denoting sickness of a partner or other trouble.

LOVE, PARTNERSHIP AND FAMILY

An attachment line that rises upwards denotes that the partner is doing well in his or her career. If a little line rises from somewhere along this line, the partner may not start out a success but he will become so later on.

A line that falls from the attachment line may indicate a partner who loses money or who loses his career.

There is an unpleasant line that some palmists call the widow line which signifies the death of a partner. It is formed when an attachment line reaches upwards to touch the crease under the little finger.

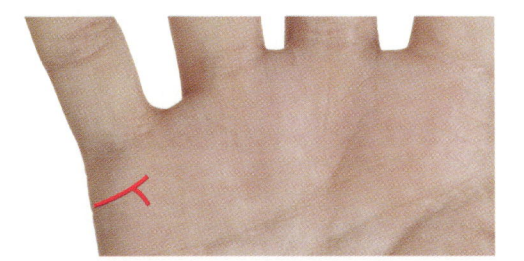

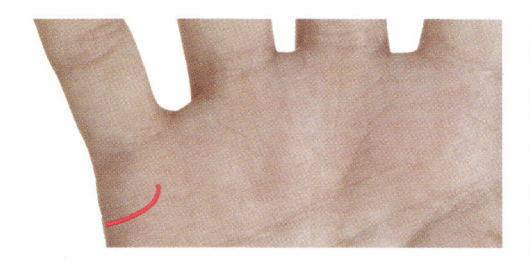

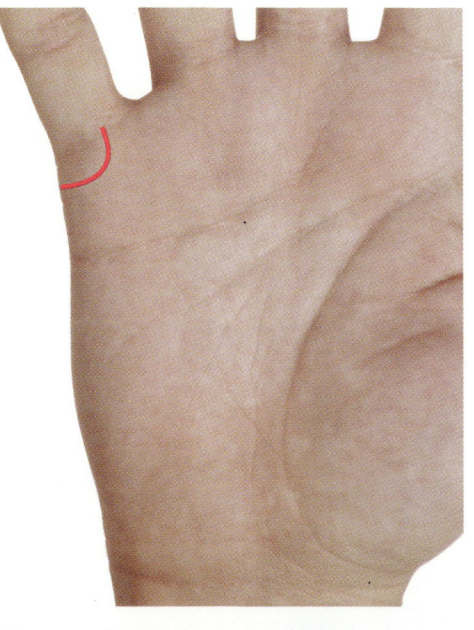

Above left: an attachment line that rises upwards denotes that the partner is doing well in his or her career.

Left: the widow line.

Far left: a line falling from the attachment line.

Below left: an attachment line that rises upwards denotes that the partner is doing well in his or her career.

LOVE, PARTNERSHIP AND FAMILY

Right: a drooping attachment line.

Below: an attachment line that droops down suggests that the partner is making life difficult for the subject.

An attachment line that droops down at the end suggests that the partner is making life difficult for the subject. We call this line the "being-put-upon line". If this touches the health line, it may indicate a health problem for either partner or it may signify a very passionate or a very troubled relationship.

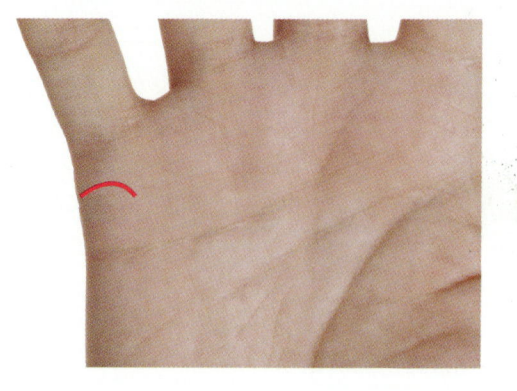

If the line is doubled or has a tiny shadow line, the partner will have other interests. These could range from being absorbed by a career or a hobby or a secondary relationship that interferes with the current relationship. In many cases, the partner is still attached to a previous partner, either for an emotional reason or a practical one such as shared children. Sometimes this line warns of an affair that is being carried on during the course of a marriage.

Right: if an attachment line is doubled or shadowed, the partner may have other interests.

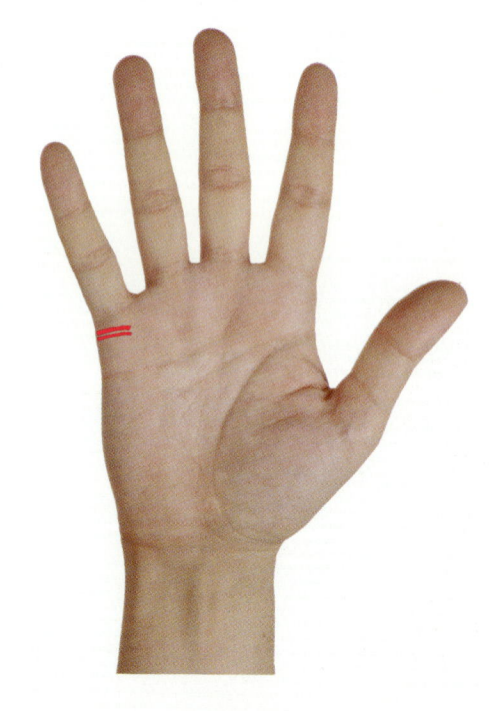

LOVE, PARTNERSHIP AND FAMILY

A line that starts out doubled, makes a V and then blends into one line suggests a strong element of friendship in the partnership and sometimes (though not always) the fact that the two people were friends for a long time before getting together.

Lines that wander into the attachment lines from some other part of the hand suggest outside interference. If these start on the mount of Venus inside the life line, crawl across the hand and then touch the attachment lines, the person's family or in-laws might be the cause of the problem. Sometimes a job gets in the way of a marriage and, in this case, a line may rise from the head line or even the fate line and touch the attachment line.

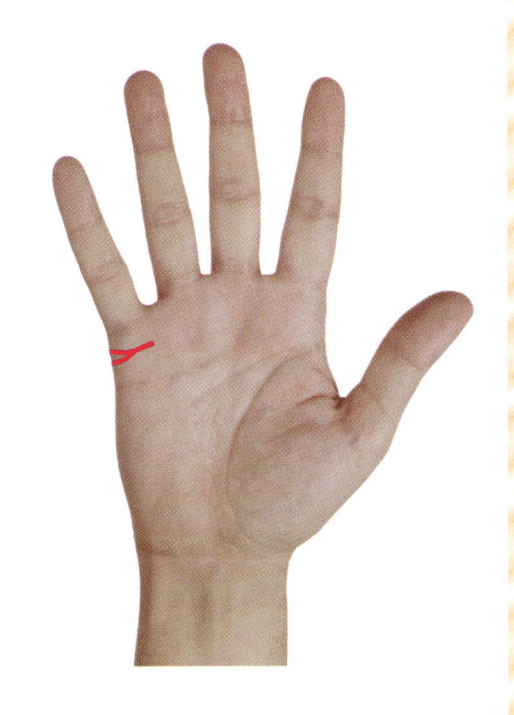

Above left: a V-shaped attachment line.

Left: a V-shaped attachment line indicates that the partnership began with friendship.

LOVE, PARTNERSHIP AND FAMILY

OTHER ISSUES

The mystic cross

Old-time palmistry books used to talk about a "mystic cross" that appeared in the middle of the hand between the heart and head lines. I have never found this to mean psychic or mystical talent, but when a line forms a cross by running diagonally downwards from the heart line and across the fate line, the marriage will be one of non-communication and it may break up without the subject ever really knowing why. Remember that a sudden end to a relationship or someone walking out without warning will also show up as an island on the heart line and a shock or disturbance on the life and fate line.

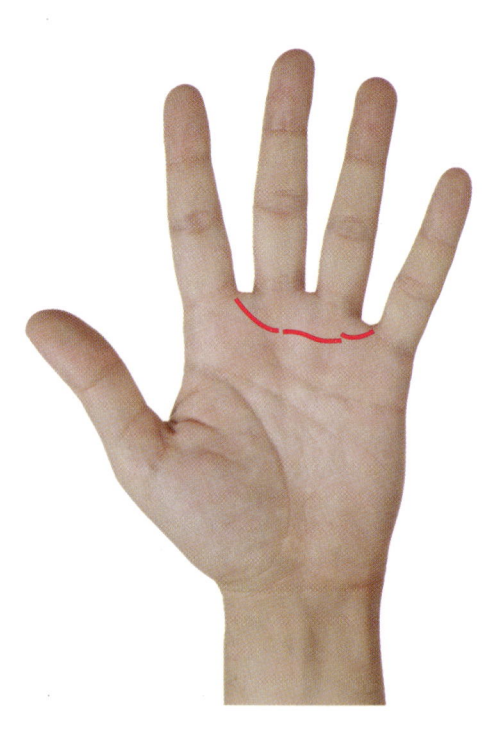

Right: the girdle of Venus.

Be careful when giving information of this kind as you could literally ruin someone's life by speaking out, and you could also be very wrong ... as I can confirm from my own experience. I have been married twice and towards the end of my 32-year first marriage, I noticed the "widow line" appearing in my own hand. It remained there after I married for the second time, then three years on my first husband died, and the line has now turned back into an ordinary attachment line.

The girdle of Venus

Another indication of a kindly, sympathetic and loving heart is the girdle of Venus. This suggests great sensitivity if it is whole, but when there is only a partial girdle the person may be interested in studying some subject that is important to him, and he will enjoy the company of friends.

LOVE, PARTNERSHIP AND FAMILY

The ring of Solomon
Although not strictly a line that concerns love, this does show wisdom and the kind of person who can listen to others and give them sensible advice.

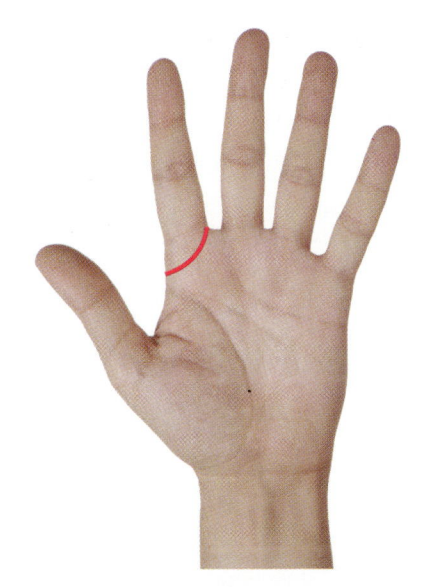

Rings of Jupiter, Saturn and Mercury
Rings that run round under one of the fingers are rare and they suggest something unusual in the personality. The ring of Jupiter runs around like a small secondary crease under the index finger and this suggests that something is blocking the person's ambitions or cramping his style. A ring of Saturn runs around under the Saturn finger and this suggests that the subject is a real misery and a loner. A ring of Mercury or an extra crease under the little finger can indicate the death of a partner, difficulties in business or such great success in business that it cuts the subject off from normal loving relationships. It may be hard to trust a person who has such a ring.

Left: the ring of Solomon.

Below left: the ring of Solomon indicates that the subject is a good listener and able to give sound advice.

LOVE, PARTNERSHIP AND FAMILY

Right: child lines running vertically through attachment lines.

Below: child lines are not accurate indicators of the number of natural children a subject may have. They can include adopted and step-children also.

Below right: islands on child lines can indicate a sick or needy child.

CHILDREN

Many people think that the attachment lines are child lines but they are not. Child lines run vertically through the attachment lines and these are notoriously difficult for even a good palmist to see or to analyse.

Child lines

Child lines are often very fine and difficult to see. It helps if you put a sprinkling of talcum powder on this area of the hand as that helps such fine lines to show up more clearly. These lines are usually on the edge of the palm where it begins to curve into the percussion side of the hand. Sometimes there are more lines than children and sometimes more children than lines, so this is not an exact science. A child that is adopted or a step-child can show up if he or she is loved, while a child who for some reason has not become part of the family or who has long since drifted away may hardly show at all.

Child lines should start at the crease which lies at the base of the little finger and then cut through the attachment lines. A line that is placed normally but that has an island on it indicates a sick or needy child. The same goes for breaks, bars that run across lines or any kind of flaking effect. These can all indicate some kind of problem concerning the relationship between the subject and the child or the condition of the child.

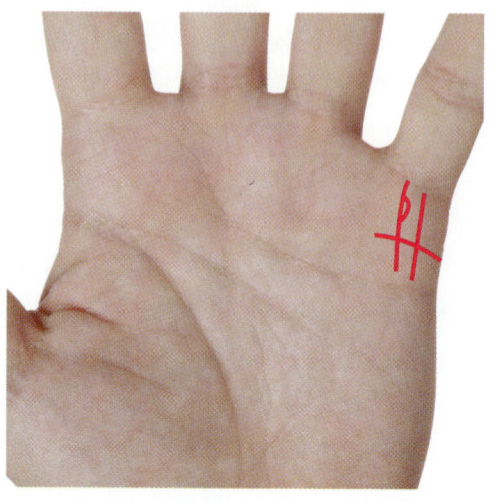

LOVE, PARTNERSHIP AND FAMILY

Generally speaking, one line means one child, two means two children and so on. Straight lines tend to mean sons while sloping ones tend to mean daughters – but don't take this too literally as a career woman may come across as a son and a gentle artist may come across as a daughter. It all really depends upon how the parent feels about the child.

If the child lines are close together, the children will be close in age while, if they are apart, there will be a gap between them. A gap may also suggest that the children are dissimilar to each other.

OTHER CIRCUMSTANCES

A person who looks after children or who teaches them will have many child lines, as long as they enjoy what they do. Much the same goes for someone who loves and keeps animals or who works with them. A high loop of humour (see page 78) also often indicates an animal lover.

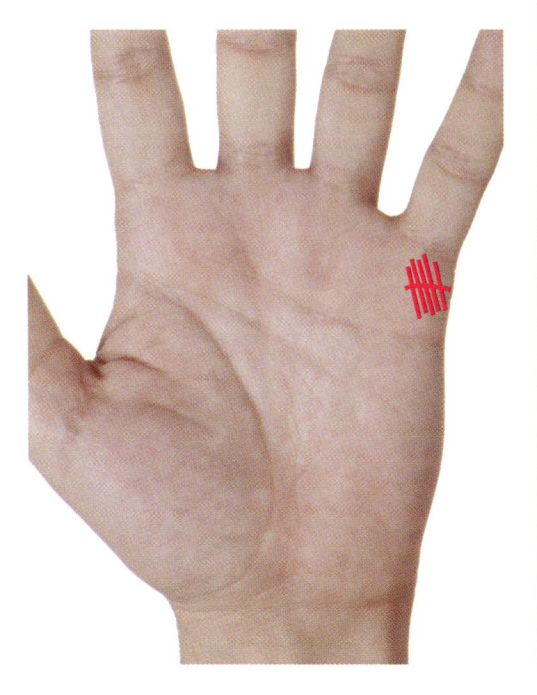

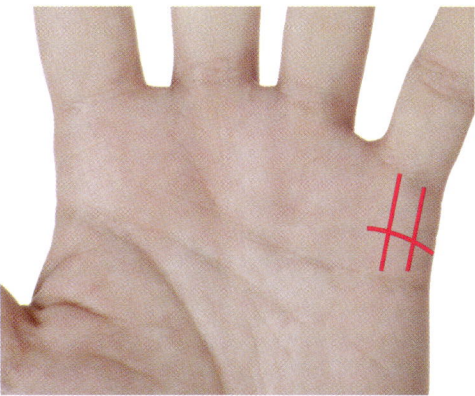

Left: each child line represents one child.

Below: if the child lines are close together, this indicates a closeness in age

Below left: multiple child lines.

LOVE, PARTNERSHIP AND FAMILY

Below: if there are no child lines at all, the subject is either far from ready to have children or he will never do so.

Right: sibling lines found on the opposite side of the hand to attachment lines.

These lines may be confusing and they may not tell the whole truth, although sometimes they tell uncomfortable truths about miscarriages and abortions. If there are no child lines at all, the subject is either far from ready to have children or he will never do so. I tend to tell people that if they have a line or two in this area of the hand that they are able to have children, but whether they choose to do so or not is up to them.

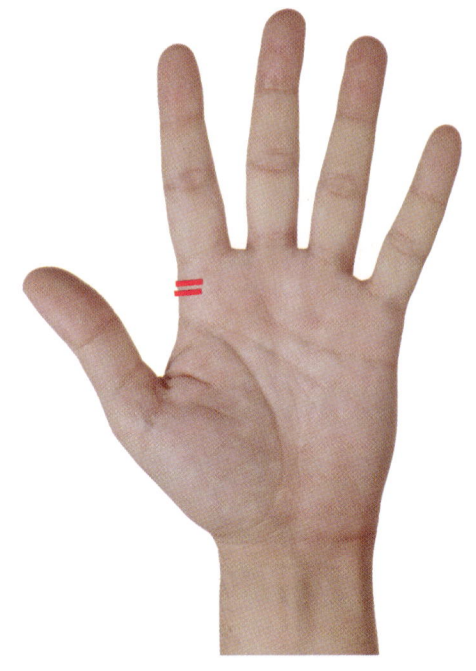

Sibling Lines

Sibling lines are found on the opposite side of the hand to attachment lines, and they refer to brothers and sisters.

These can be read in more or less the same way as attachment lines, e.g. two lines suggest two brothers and sisters (or similar close relationships). Such marks as islands, stars on the lines, breaks etc. all suggest that a brother or sister has a problem.

LOVE, PARTNERSHIP AND FAMILY

Left: two sibling lines indicate two brothers and sisters etc. in the same way as child lines.

Fate, Fortune and Fame

In this chapter we will look at the fate line, the Apollo line and the health line plus few other less important lines, and it is here that you will run into the fundamental problem with palmistry. If you give an astrologer a birth chart to work on, he can count on finding all the planets and other features laid out in front of him and it is only his own level of skill and knowledge that drives him on or holds him back. Hand reading is not as straightforward. Lines may be as clear as a railway map, or they can be broken up, displaced, doubled or missing, and there may be stray lines that don't appear in any book on palmistry but that must have something important to say. Even in the best of circumstances, the fate and Apollo lines are like irregular verbs because, even if everything else on a hand is absolutely normal, these two are bound to be all over the place. This doesn't make life easy for a professional palmist, let alone for a beginner.

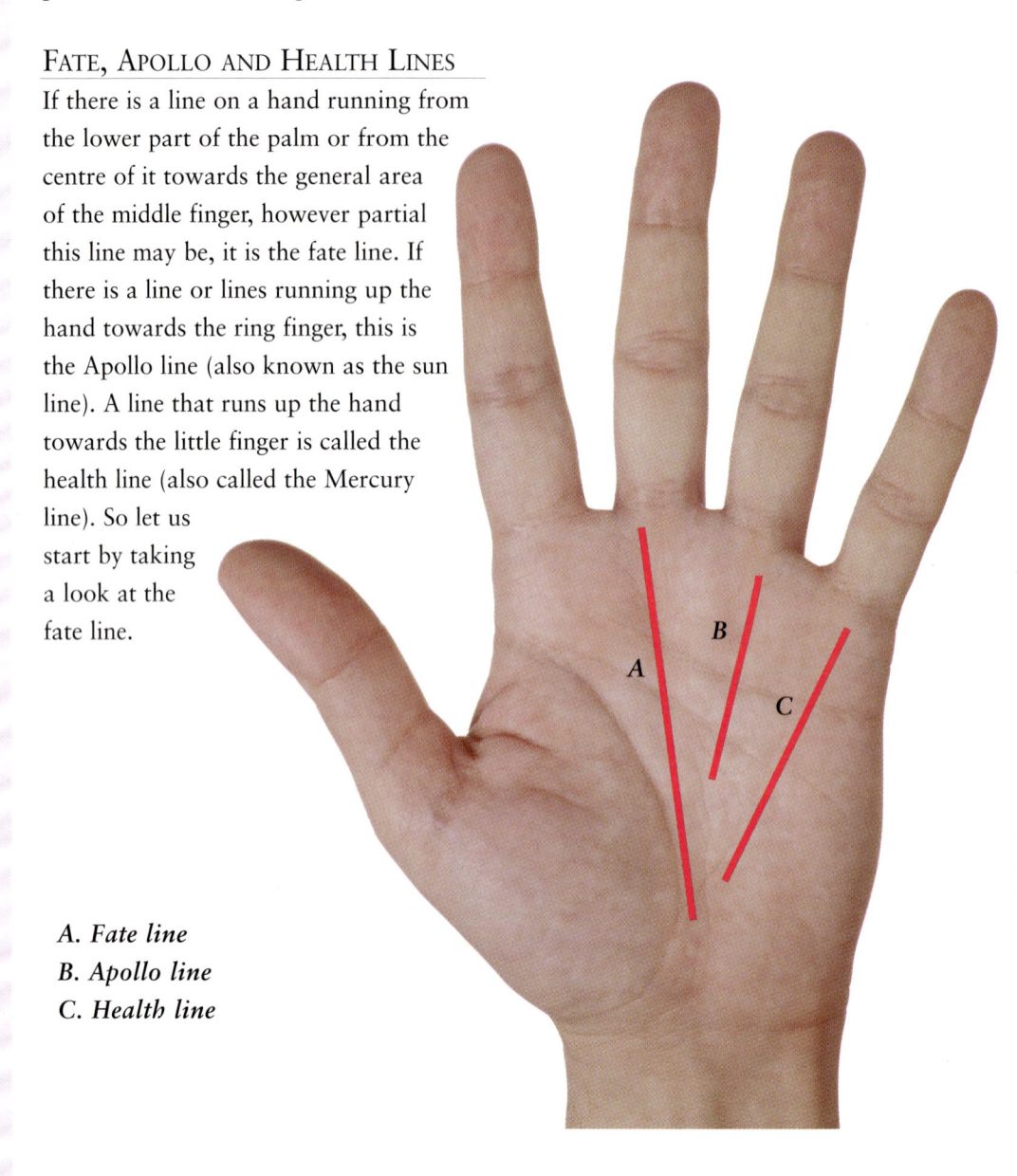

Fate, Apollo and Health Lines

If there is a line on a hand running from the lower part of the palm or from the centre of it towards the general area of the middle finger, however partial this line may be, it is the fate line. If there is a line or lines running up the hand towards the ring finger, this is the Apollo line (also known as the sun line). A line that runs up the hand towards the little finger is called the health line (also called the Mercury line). So let us start by taking a look at the fate line.

A. *Fate line*
B. *Apollo line*
C. *Health line*

FATE, FORTUNE AND FAME

THE FATE LINE

The fate line runs more or less up the middle of the hand from somewhere around the lower end of the palm towards the middle finger or to some point either side of it. A fate line can be as long and strong as any of the other lines on the hand or it can be faint or there may be parts of it that start and stop at various points along the hand, or there may be no real fate line at all.

The presence of any kind of fate line suggests that at least something happens during the course of a person's life. He may give too much time and energy to others and to doing his duty, but at least he is doing something, and the chances are that he will find a way of life that works for him and then stick to it. Someone with no fate line is either born with a silver spoon in his mouth or he never really makes an effort. If the line starts out strongly towards the lower end of the hand and then peters out, the subject either has a tough start in life and then coasts along during the rest of it, or he loses control of his life in some way. A very common scenario is where the fate line only starts half way up the hand and then continues upwards, and this shows that the subject reaches a point where he begins to make things happen or where things start to happen to him.

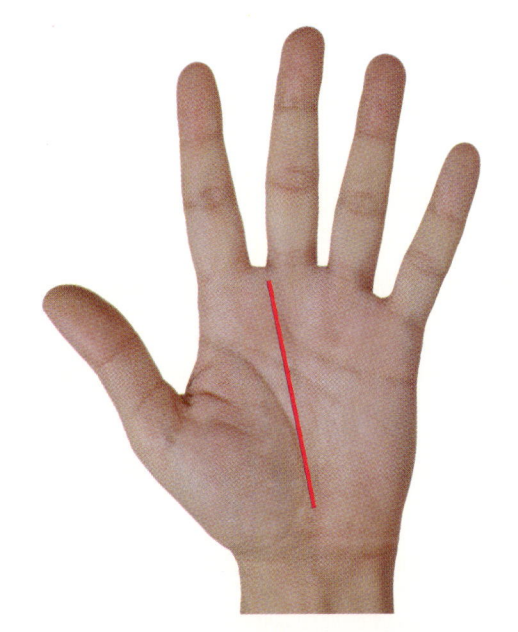

Left: the fate line runs up the centre of the hand.

Below: someone with no fate line is either born with a silver spoon in his mouth or he never really makes an effort.

FATE, FORTUNE AND FAME

Timing on the fate line

Up to now, I have avoided talking about timing on the hand because it is so difficult to assess. An event that stands out in the mind can show up as a long island on any line and this can give the impression that the event went on for years, while in reality the upset came and went in a relatively short period of time, although its effects remain in the person's mind long after. This kind of scenario is especially common on the minor hand because it registers the way we feel about something rather than the actual facts of the case.

It would be nice if all the lines on the hand were like a road where all one has to do is measure it and see where the turnings, traffic lights and traffic islands are in order to assess the timing of events, but this is not the case. The only lines that give a reasonably dependable timing mechanism are the life, fate and Apollo lines. In the case of the fate line, a very rough guide is that life up to the age of around 30 or 35 is shown on the fate line from the lower end of the hand up to the point where it meets the head line. If the head line slopes down the hand and is, therefore, rather low, the fate line will cross it at around the age of 30. If it is high and runs straight across the hand, the age at which the fate line crosses it is more like 35. The same goes for the point where the fate line crosses the heart line. If the heart line is deep, this event will occur at around the age of 40; if it is high, then 45 is more likely.

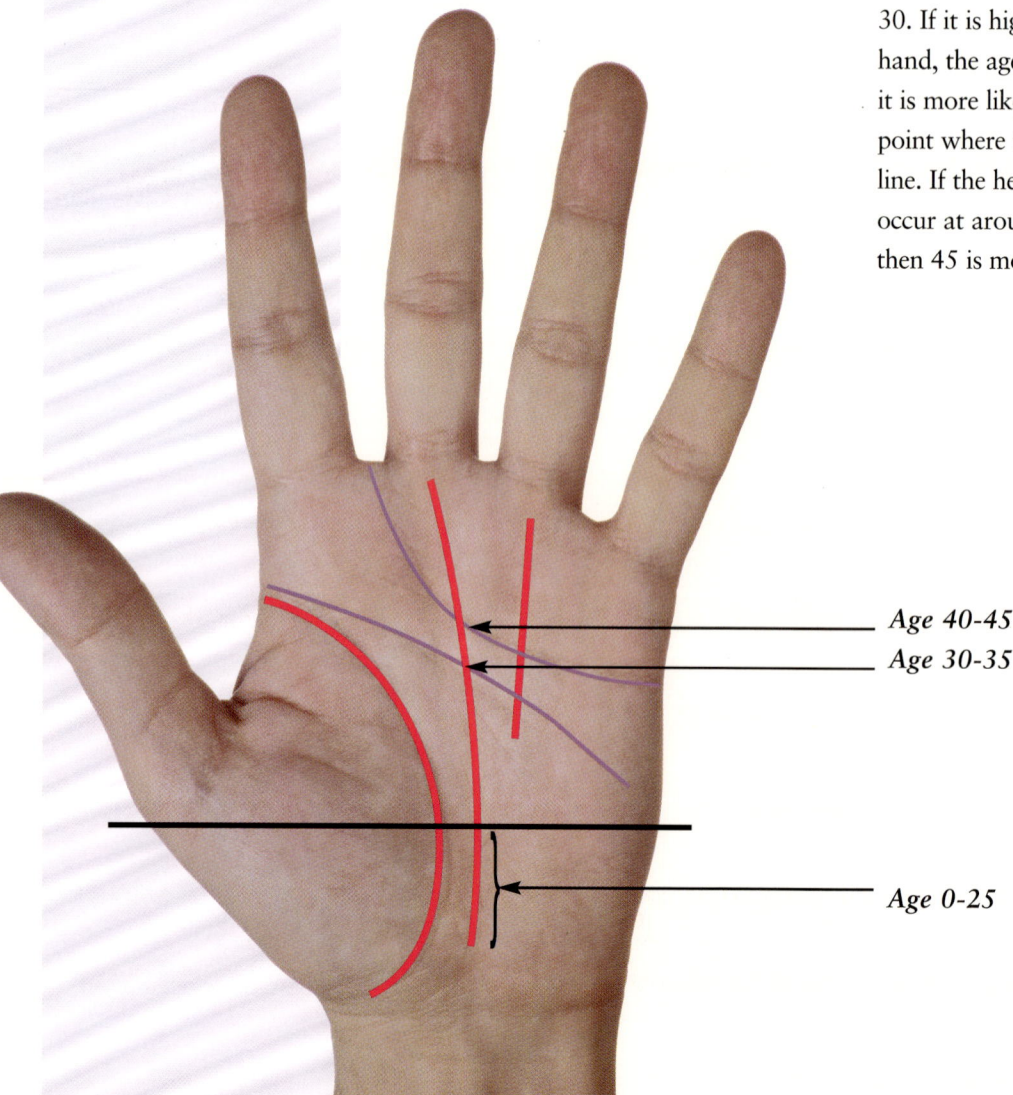

Below: timing on the fate line.

Age 40-45
Age 30-35
Age 0-25

FATE, FORTUNE AND FAME

The remaining years are shown in the small area above the heart line. In days gone by, ordinary people were lucky to live to middle age, so there was less need for room on the hand to show events in later life.

The fate line gives information on important people entering and leaving our lives, times of advancement and setback, the way we work or run our homes and times of stability or change. It is indeed the line of our fate.

The lower end of the fate line
Take a pen or ruler and lay it across the hand where the knuckle that joins the thumb to the hand is. Track across and see if there is any fate line below this point. The line below this point shows events up to roughly the age of 25.

Below: later years are indicated above the heart line. In days gone by little room was needed here as people were lucky to live beyond middle age.

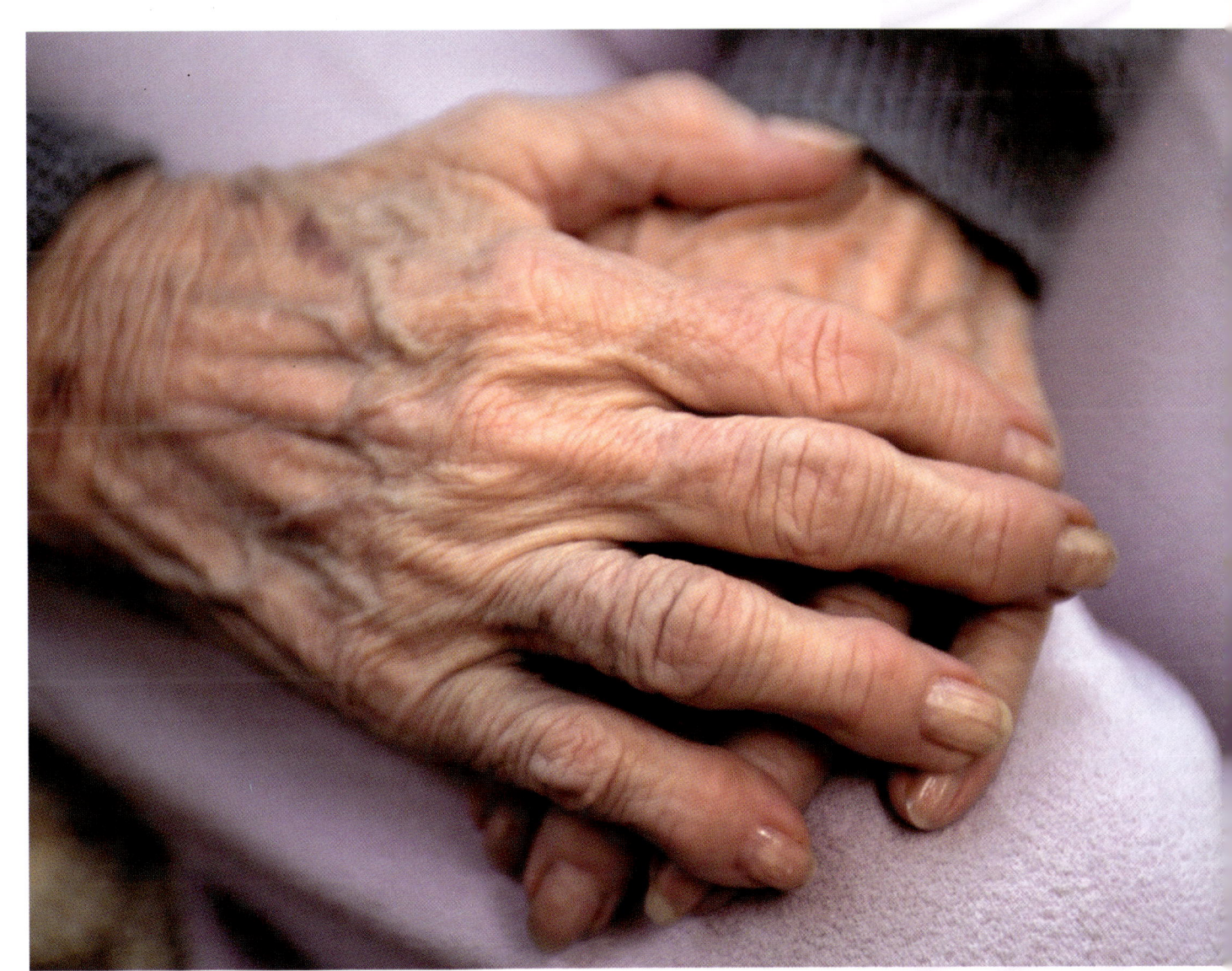

FATE, FORTUNE AND FAME

The start of the fate line
If the fate line starts in the lower half of the palm, however faint, it suggests that the subject had a variety of events to live through early in life. If it starts on or within the life line, the subject's family helped him to make headway in life, possibly by giving him a good education and much encouragement. If it is quite tied to the life line or a line that branches off the life, the family's influence might have been too strong for comfort.

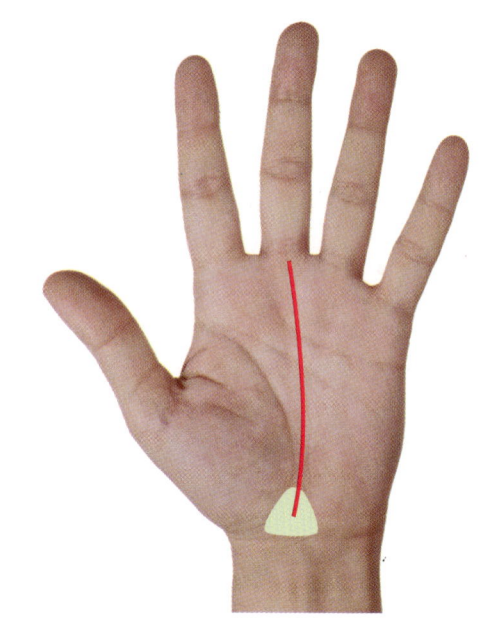

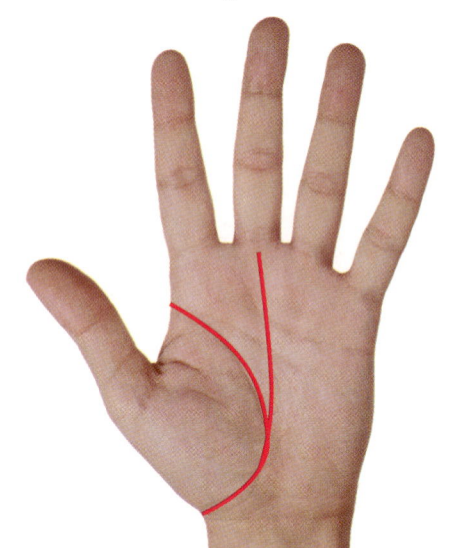

Right: a fate line tied to the life line.

Above right: a fate line starting on the mount of Neptune.

Below right: lower end of the fate line is part of a displaced life line.

A fate line that starts in the central area on the mount of Neptune shows that the person can count on family approval, but that he is also free to make his own decisions. A fate line that starts on the mount of the Moon suggests that the family are not influential in the subject's early life and that it is outsiders who give him the most help. If there is no fate line in this area, the subject probably drifts along for a while without doing very much or without making crucial decisions or taking important actions.

Sometimes the lower end of the fate line is also part of a displaced life line. In this case, you should read the same line twice; once downwards for life line information and once upwards for fate line information. This can also be an indication that the subject's parents had some influence over the way his life went in the early years and that they may also remain influential as life progresses. Stray lines that wander across the fate line at the lowest end can indicate family problems that affected the person during childhood (also check the condition of the start of the life line).

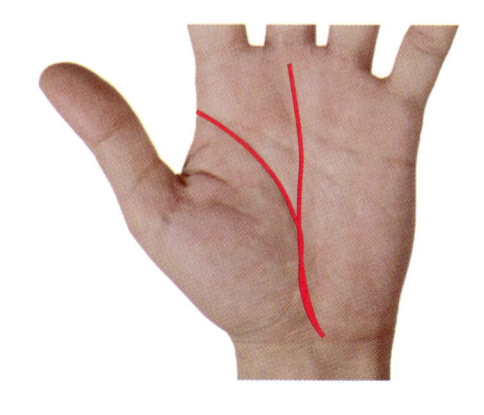

FATE, FORTUNE AND FAME

Branching fate line

If a small branch joins the fate line in these early stages, the chances are that the subject made an important marriage-type relationship very early on. If such a joining branch stays put, so to speak, the marriage also stays put, but if a branch later peels away from the fate line a little higher up, the chances are that that early marriage didn't last. Islands that appear in this area suggest periods of difficulty and confusion, which may relate to romantic problems or early educational or career problems (check heart and head lines for confirmation).

Now progress up the line and see what else may be marked there. The following will show you a few common features:

Islands on the fate line

Islands on any part of the fate line indicate split energies, so the subject may feel torn in two directions or he may be coping with any number of problems or setbacks.

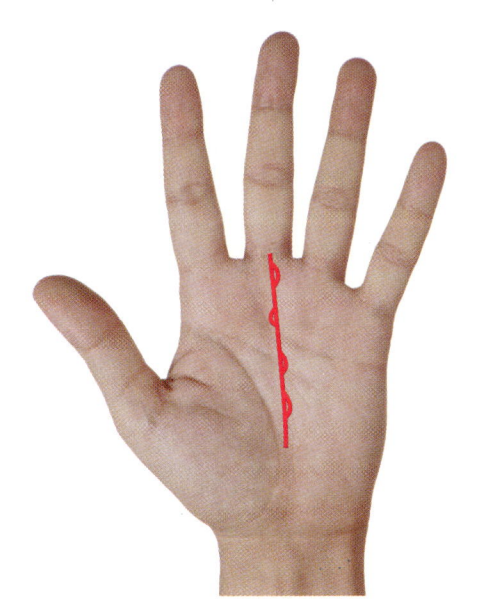

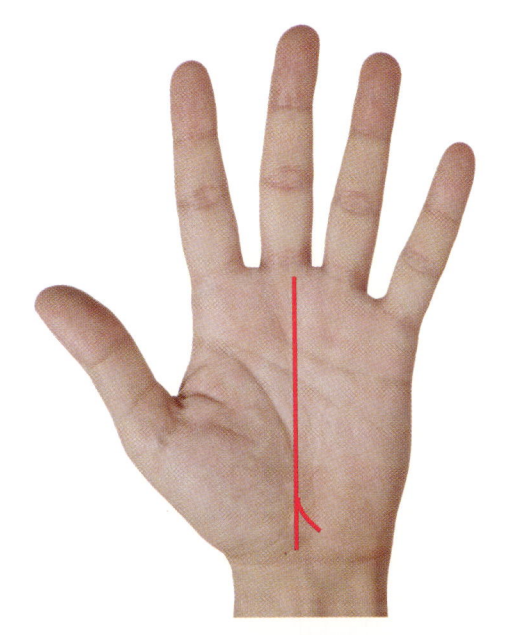

Left: branching on the fate line.

Below left: islands on the fate line

Below: islands on the fate line indicate being torn between two directions.

FATE, FORTUNE AND FAME

Right: a jumping fate line, indicating a change in direction.

Jumping fate line
If the fate line stops and then starts again slightly to the left or the right of the original line this indicates a change of direction. If the line jumps towards the radial (thumb) side of the hand, the subject will put his energies into a career, but if it jumps towards the r (percussion) side of the hand, domestic and family life will prevail. The line may jump back again at some later point, showing yet another change of direction.

Bars, breaks and stars on the fate line
If the fate line fades out for a while, the subject will go through a quiet period until it starts up again. Bars, breaks, stars, crosses or any other interference on the fate line denotes setbacks. A line that ends in a small fork and then starts up again suggests a change of career or a change of direction. In this case, the subject may even walk away from a job and then go on to do something completely different.

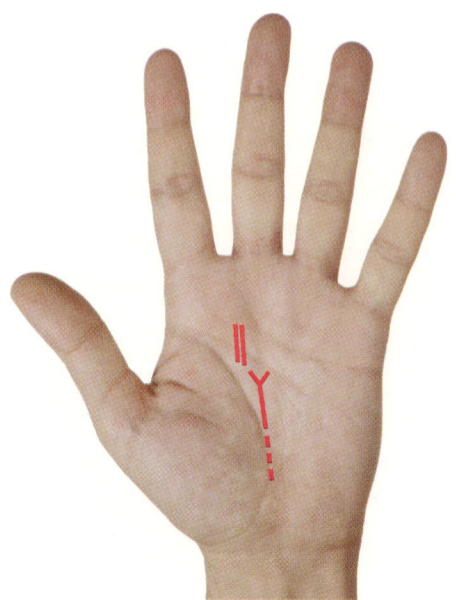

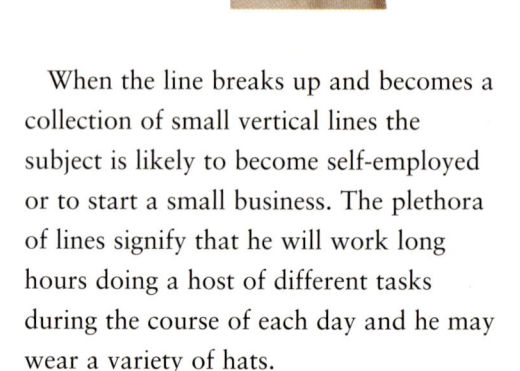

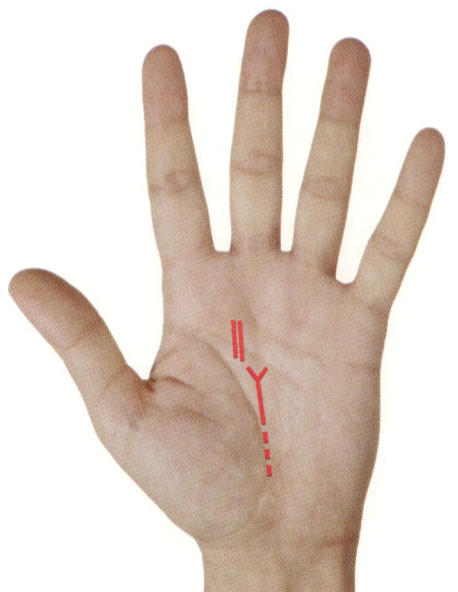

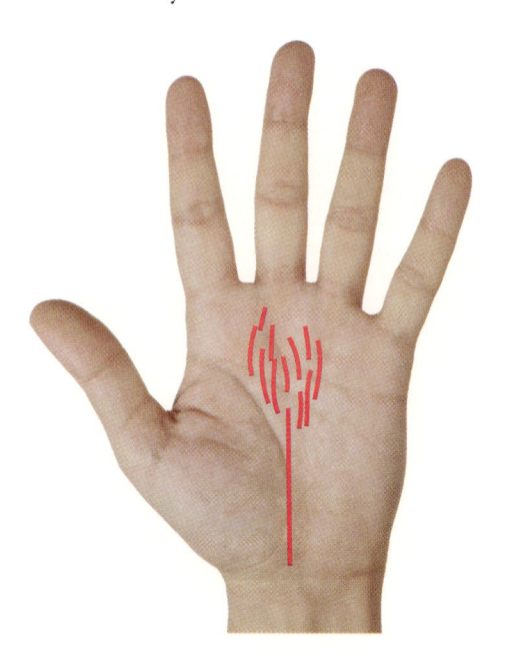

When the line breaks up and becomes a collection of small vertical lines the subject is likely to become self-employed or to start a small business. The plethora of lines signify that he will work long hours doing a host of different tasks during the course of each day and he may wear a variety of hats.

Right: bars and breaks on the fate line.

Far right: a fading fate line.

FATE, FORTUNE AND FAME

Endings on the fate line

Now, look at the upper end of the fate line and see where and how it ends. If the fate line travels towards the index finger or the space between the index and middle finger and becomes part of the heart line, the subject will put his heart into his job or business. It also suggests a fair amount of luck and good fortune later in life.

If the line marches up to the middle finger, the subject will not be short of money in old age, although he may have to work hard for this during the course of his life. The chances are that the line divides into two, is joined by other pieces of line or is in a number of pieces by this time. The more pieces, the harder the subject's life is and the harder he works, but if he can find a way of making life a little easier for himself, the extra pieces of line may fade, leaving one or two stronger traces. If there are many lines here, the subject could wear himself out with work.

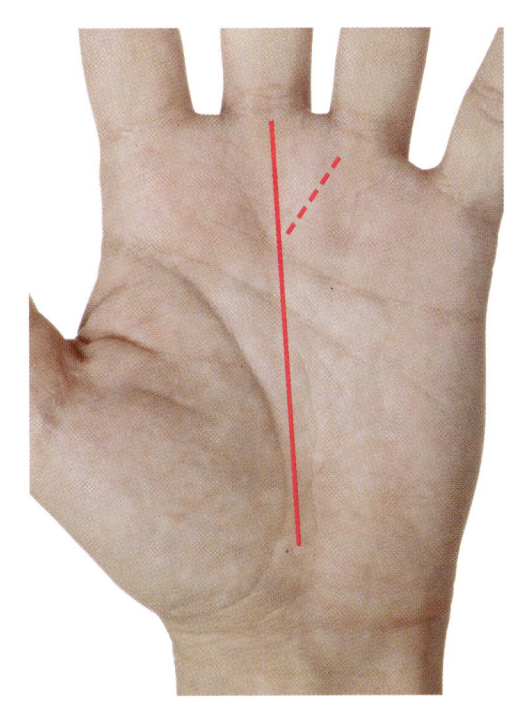

If the fate line or a branch of it travels towards the Apollo finger, the subject can expect his later life to be jolly, and he will be able to afford to have fun rather than to work himself to death.

Left: different endings on the fate line.

Below left: a fate line which ends towards the Apollo finger indicates that the subject will be happy in later life and will not have to work all the time.

FATE, FORTUNE AND FAME

THE APOLLO LINE

This travels up the hand towards the Apollo finger but, more often than not, the only part of this line that can actually be found on a hand is under the Apollo finger stretching upwards from the area of the heart line. If there is a more complete Apollo line a number of possibilities apply. Firstly, the person may live much of his life in the public eye as a performer or an artist. The subject will certainly be creative and, if this is added to a curved head line, a creative career is definitely indicated. The start of this line will show whether the subject receives help from his family (closer to the middle of the hand or the life line) or whether it is outsiders who see his value (starting on the mount of the Moon).

All the usual things apply to this line; therefore, breaks, jumps, islands and lines that interfere with it all suggest setbacks or breaks in the train of the person's life.

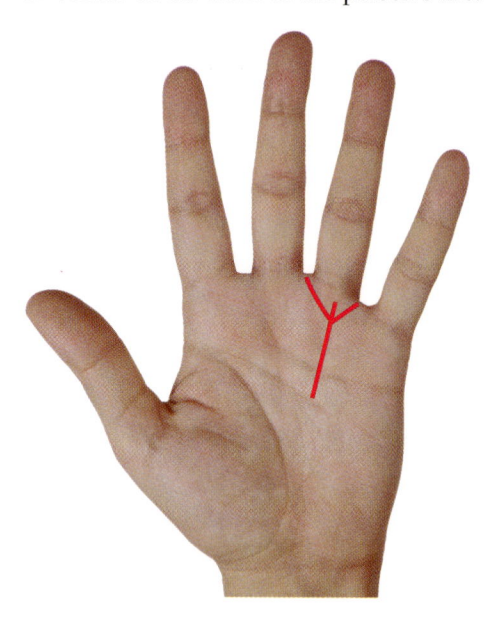

A trident on the mount of Apollo
This line also has something to say about buying property, so a strong patch of Apollo line indicates buying a house and a period of happy home life to follow. If there is a strong line at the upper end on the mount of Apollo, the subject will be happy and comfortable in old age. A trident effect at the very top end indicates that the subject will always be able to count on luck, inheritance and/or the ability to make money.

To double check this, look at the edge of the hand on the radial (thumb) side for a "money-maker" line that runs vertically towards the side of the mount of Jupiter.

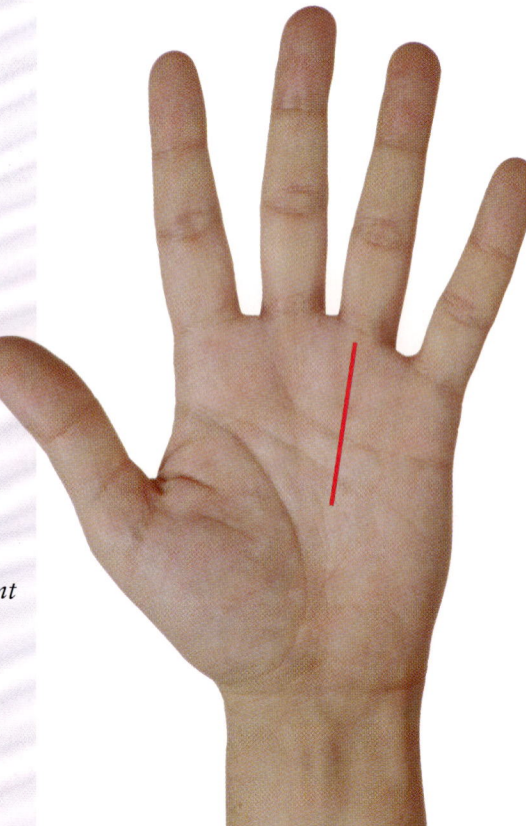

Right: the Apollo line.

Above right: a trident on the mount of Apollo.

Far right: a money-maker line.

FATE, FORTUNE AND FAME

A piece of Apollo close to Saturn

A whole or a partial piece of Apollo line at the top of the hands under the fingers suggests domestic security in old age. If this line is close to the mount of Saturn, the subject will live close to his family, if it is closer to the mount of Mercury, he will live closer to his friends or in some place that has a personal attachment for him.

If the line ends in a long V, he will take care of a parent and he may have the parent living with him for a while. If it ends in a "ladder of success", he will make it in the end, despite setbacks.

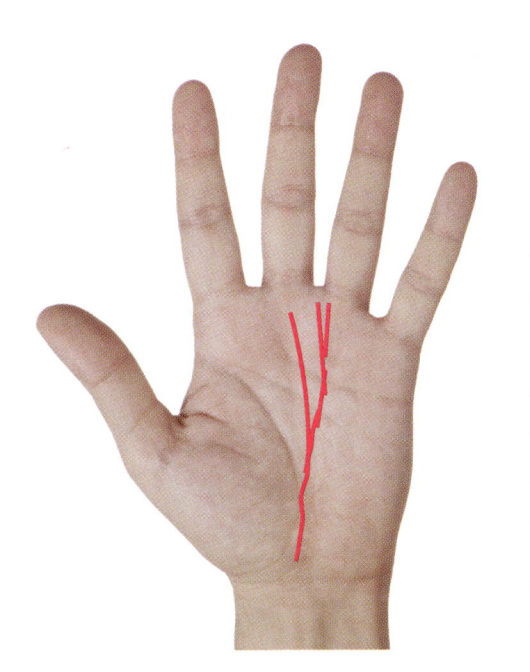

Left: the Apollo line ending in a long V.

Below: if the Apollo line is close to the mount of Saturn, the subject will live close to his family in later years.

Right: the health line.

Below right: a curved health line indicating an extremely intuitive subject.

FATE, FORTUNE AND FAME

THE HEALTH LINE

Some palmists call this the line of Mercury, but sometimes there is a double line and palmists will refer to one as the health line and the other as the line of Mercury. It doesn't really matter either way. The presence of this line does not mean that the person will be sickly during his life, but it does show that he may be interested in helping or healing others. This may manifest itself in his choice of profession or simply by looking after his family or others. If the health line is badly chained, the chances are that he will spend a fair part of his life looking after a sick partner.

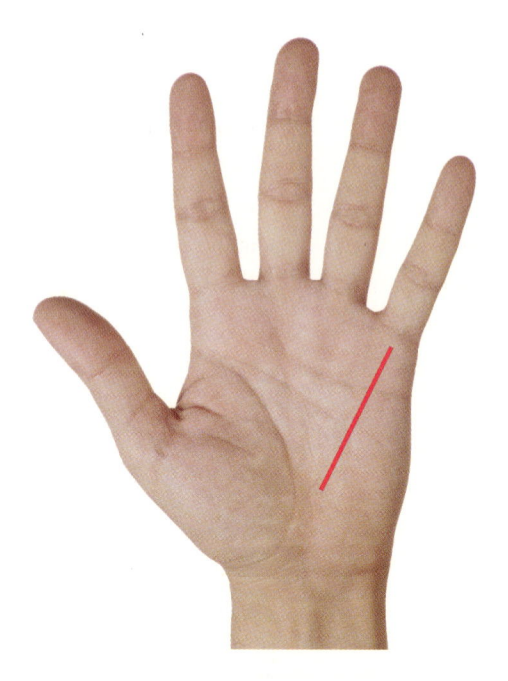

Straight health line

If it runs straight towards the mount of Mercury, he will help others by communicating with them. A counsellor or a writer of self-help books would have such a line.

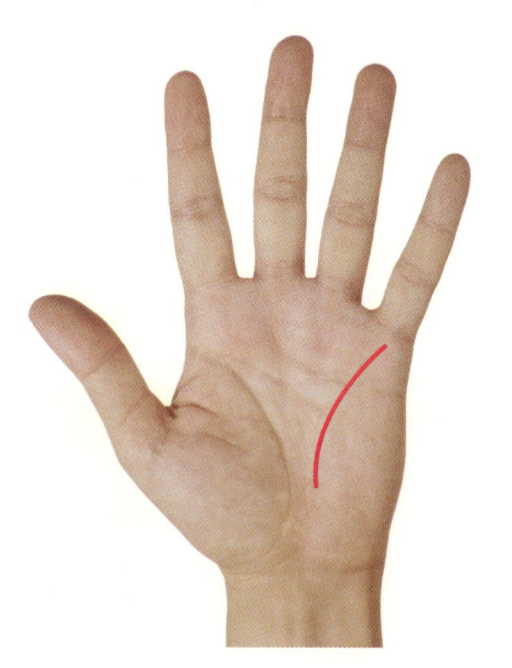

Curved health line

If this line is curved, the subject will be extremely intuitive and probably clairvoyant or psychic and he may be a natural, spiritual or psychic healer.

If it ends in healing striate, he will definitely become involved in some form of healing, either "normal" or "spiritual" healing. By the way, the word "striate" is pronounced striata. In some cases, the health line ends in a curve that touches an attachment line. This shows that some form of passion or obsession is put into a relationship.

FATE, FORTUNE AND FAME

Healing striate

There are very few cut and dried marks on the hand, but this is one that palmists always take into account. The healing mark is a strange affair of three parallel lines which lie on a slight diagonal on the mount of Mercury and they are crossed by another diagonal line. This mark shows that the subject has healing powers which may be of the purely spiritual kind or they may be used along with regular medical training.

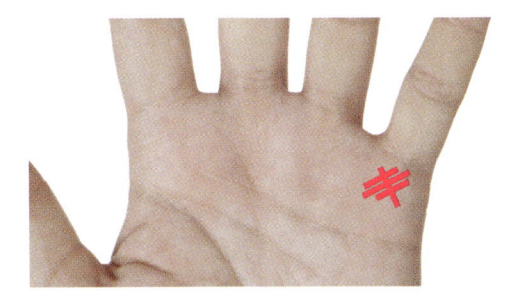

Much the same can be said for a counsellor, although check to see if there is also a ring or line of Solomon on the mount of Jupiter (see back to page 59).

Left: healing striate on the mount of Mercury.

The marks	What they mean
	Three slightly diagonal lines are the most common type of healing or medical striate. One line in this area indicates that the subject can work alone. One, two, three, or four lines signify someone who works one-to-one with people.
	The presence of many fine lines suggests working in a group. A line that touches the heart line and another that touches the lower end of the finger suggest that the subject is a teacher and a communicator. If a line reaches into the corner of the Mercury finger, the subject is psychic.
	A long fork on the Apollo side suggests that the subject saves people. This person may be a nurse in casualty or intensive care, a surgeon or a healer.
	A long line with a V formation on the top belongs on the hands of those who work with terminally ill people. Their job, is, unconsciously perhaps, to "lift souls", that is to help them pass from this world to the next. This V formulation can be found on the hands of, for example, hospice staff.
	A long fork on the percussion side, near the attachment lines, shows that the subject cares for children. He or she may foster, adopt or work with children.

Marks and Loops

Asian and Oriental palmists lend more credence to stray marks on the hand than Western palmists do and they use these in much the same way as a tea-leaf reader would use the shapes and symbols that form among the leaves in a tea cup. In short, this allows for a semi-clairvoyant kind of reading. However, even scientific palmists take a few stray marks on board when they come across them.

Marks	What they mean	What they look like
Square unlucky	Restriction. On head line, work problems. On heart line, emotional restriction. On life line, could be protection or restriction.	
Square lucky	Protection, from danger, harm, loss, depending upon which line it covers.	
Triangle	Talent. Look at placement. For example, may be a great sailor if on Luna.	
Star unlucky	Supposed to be a truly malevolent sign. If the star is red, there will be a severe problem. See the location on the hand to work out the problem.	
Star lucky	On the mount of Jupiter: wealth through achievement. If on this mount and close to the heart line: the subject will marry money. On Apollo: fame and fortune.	
Grilles	These may not be easy to spot but, if you see one, it always indicates illness or trouble in the appropriate area.	

MARKS AND LOOPS

A cross on Apollo and the Moon
A cross or a star draws attention to the mount it is on or to the line that it touches. Such marks are considered lucky by some, unlucky by others. A cross on the mount of Apollo suggests a win or a windfall. A cross on the mount of the Moon suggests safety while travelling.

A grille is a strange mark that appears during illness, but I will come back to this in the health section of this book.

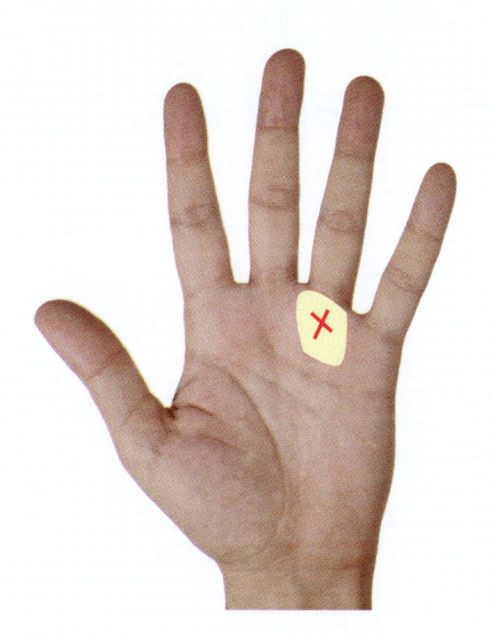

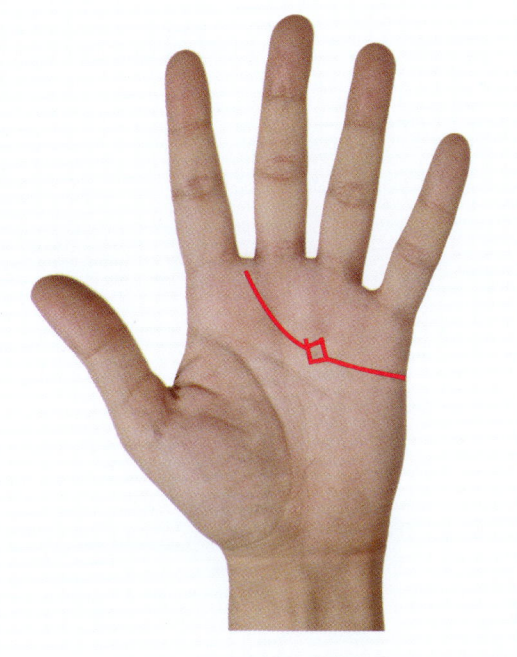

Left: a square on the heart line.

Far left: a cross on Apollo.

Below left: a square on the life line.

A triangle is said to be a sign of talent. A square is always taken on board as it shows restriction but also protection. For example, a square on the mount of Jupiter would suggest some restriction in a person's ambitions which may be due to outside circumstances or to low self-esteem. A square on the heart line can indicate a tough time in a relationship, loneliness, a restricted love life and so on. However, a square that surrounds a break in any line is a kind of bandage that helps the person to recover from illness or from some other setback.

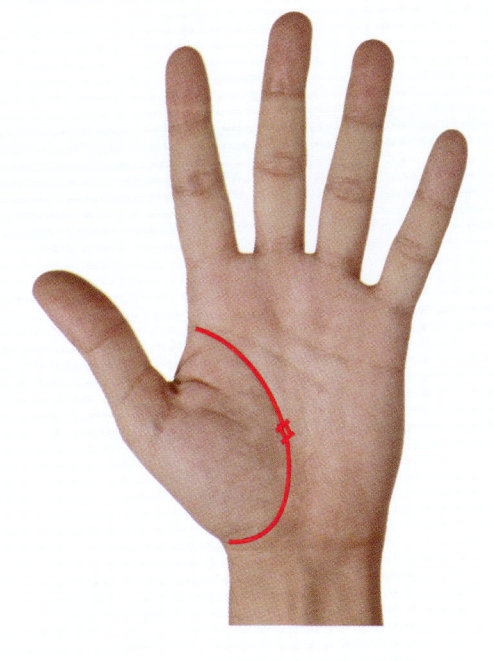

MARKS AND LOOPS

Loops
There are various skin ridge patters which are similar to fingerprints that may or may not appear in a hand.

What the loops represent
The loop of humour shows a sense of humour and often a love of animals.

The loop of style shows dress sense and an eye for colour and décor.

The loop of serious intent shows a capacity for hard work.

The Rajah loop shows royal blood – seriously, it does!

The memory loop shows a good memory for names, dates etc.

The ulnar loop shows a love of the countryside and of nature.

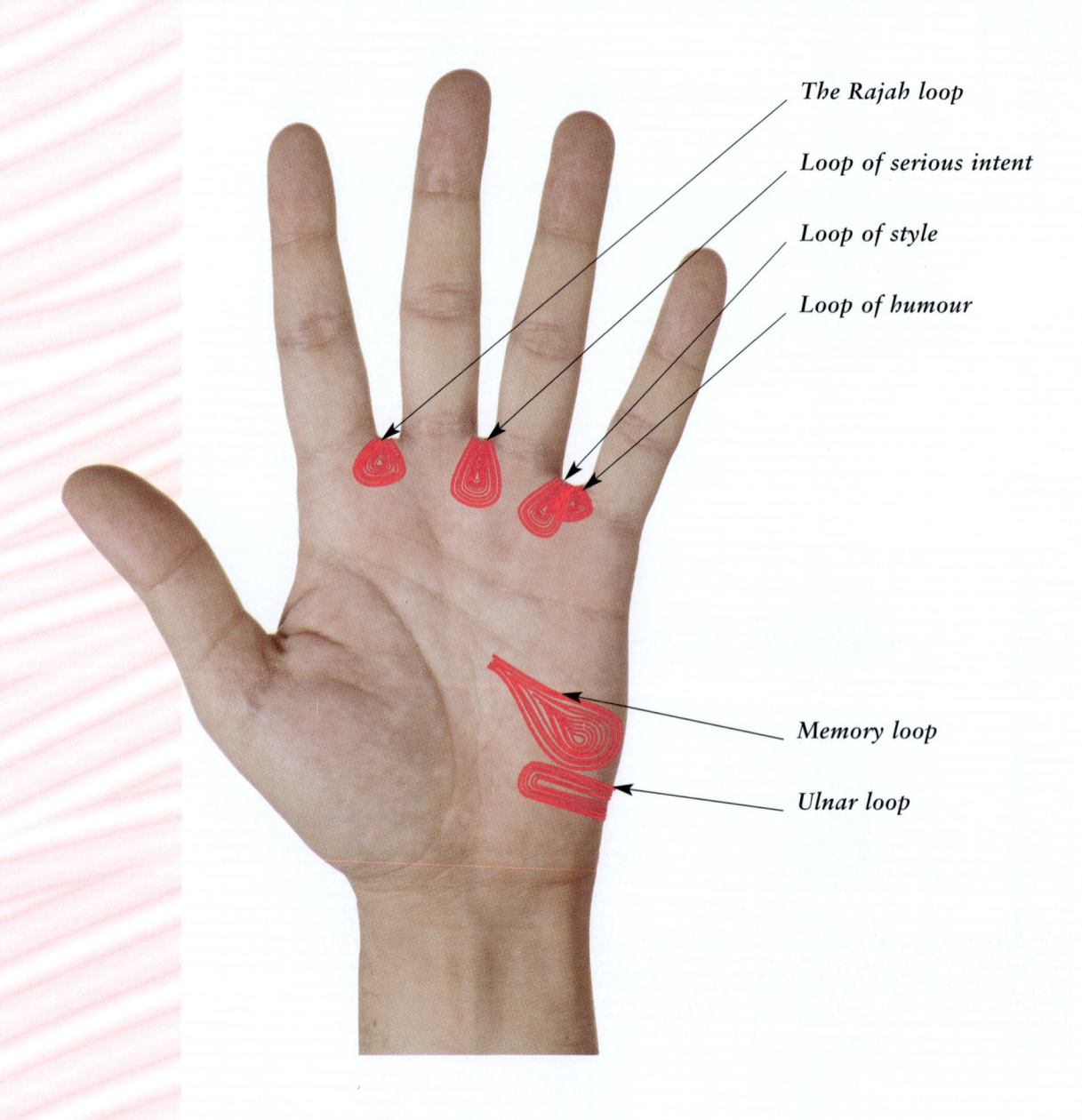

The Rajah loop

Loop of serious intent

Loop of style

Loop of humour

Memory loop

Ulnar loop

MARKS AND LOOPS

Left: the ulnar loop shows a love of the countryside and of nature.

MARKS AND LOOPS

Travel lines

Travel lines appear on the percussion side of the hand, all the way down from the crease of the heart line to the bottom of the hand. These can be numerous or few, strong or faint. If there are many faint lines, the person will make many trips but none will have special significance. However, any outstanding line suggests that a particular journey will stand out in the subject's mind.

The following list applies to everybody, wherever they happen to have been born. Roughly speaking, trips to northern latitudes are shown in the upper part of the percussion, with Scandinavia being a strong contender. Europe is shown next and Mediterranean countries beneath this, but usually still marginally above the head line. Canada and America are sited around or a little below the end of the

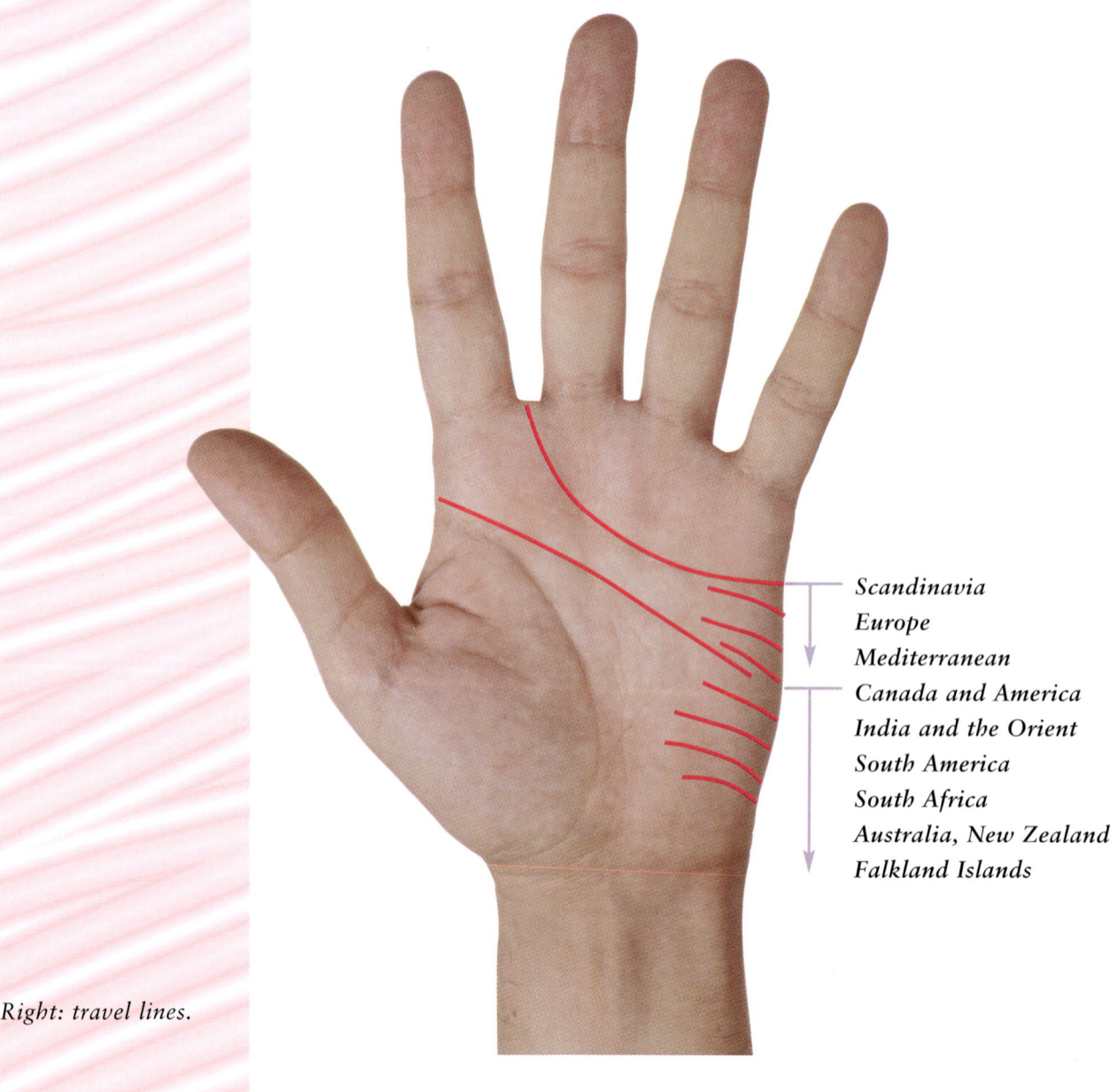

Scandinavia
Europe
Mediterranean
Canada and America
India and the Orient
South America
South Africa
Australia, New Zealand
Falkland Islands

Right: travel lines.

MARKS AND LOOPS

head line, with India and the Orient beneath. South America, South Africa follow next with Australia, New Zealand and the Falkland Islands or other southerly latitudes at the bottom. A strong line coming in from the side of the hand on the mount of the Moon can point to an important journey. It is quite common to have a strong line here that has nothing to do with travel but which means that the subject suffers from allergies, but this is more likely to be the case when the hand is very creased and lined than if it is fairly empty of line.

Left: if there are many faint lines, the person will make many trips but none will have special significance.

MARKS AND LOOPS

Branched travel lines
If a travel line touches or throws a branch to the life line, it suggests that friends, relatives or other contacts are the cause of travel. If a travel line touches or throws a branch to the head line, it suggests travel in connection with work.

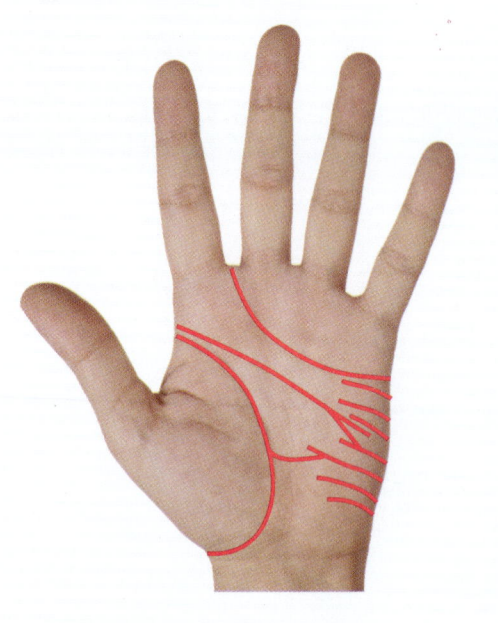

Above right: broken, islanded and frayed travel lines.

Right: branched travel lines.

Far right: if a travel line touches or throws a branch to the head line, it suggests travel in connection with work.

Islands, breaks and frays on travel lines
Look closely at these lines to see if they are in a good condition or if there is an island, a break, a frayed effect or any other disturbance on any of them as this will indicate problems or other events while the subject is away from home.

MARKS AND LOOPS

Left: travel lines can be extremely accurate in pinpointing exactly where in the world the subject has visited, and whether or not the trip was significant to them.

I remember on one occasion when dealing with a client that I found my eye being drawn to a small star on the upper edge of a travel line. I took a chance and asked the client whether she had ever been to Canada, and she told me that she had fairly recently returned from a trip there. The star was about two-thirds along the line, counting it from the edge of the hand. I took another chance and asked if she had been to Toronto. She was amazed at this comment and agreed that she had indeed been in Toronto. A small vertical line passed through the travel line just to the right of the star so I took another chance and suggested that she had stayed half way up Yonge Street on the left hand side a few blocks to the north of the Eaton Centre. Once again my client confirmed this – and by now we were both astounded! I then asked her what had been so significant about this trip and she told me that she had met an important new lover there.

HEALTH ON THE HANDS

This is a huge subject and I can only touch on the basics in a book of this size. In the days before medical diagnosis became as intensely mechanised as it is today, doctors used far more folk or casual knowledge to assess a person's health. They looked at the eyes, the tongue and the hands to assess symptoms of common ailments.

Right: obviously the hands of an elderly person, but the discoloration indicates heart and circulatory problems.

Below: the condition of hands can also indicate pregnancy.

THE COLOUR OF HANDS

The colour of the hands can give an indication of the general health: yellow signifying liver problems; the red palms of the smoker; blue/grey/mauve fingers suggesting heart and circulatory problems.

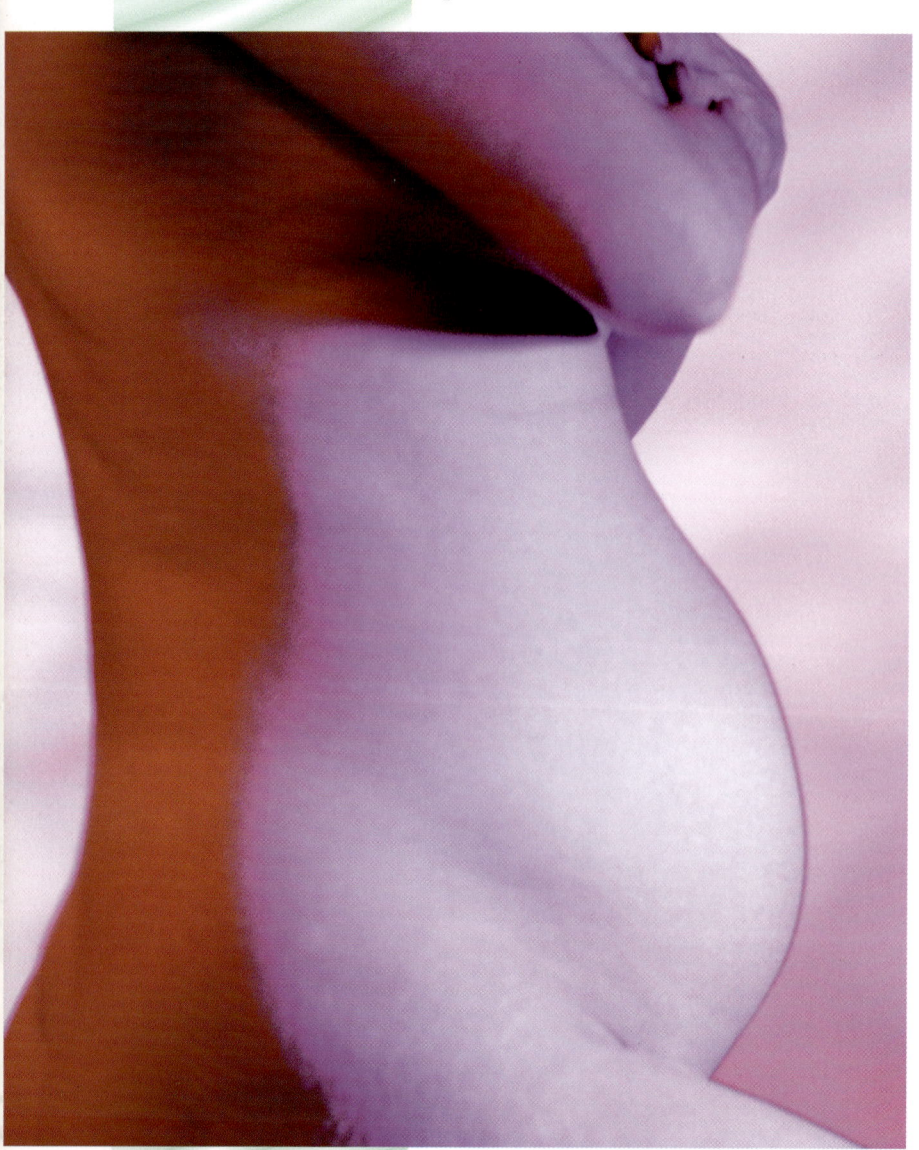

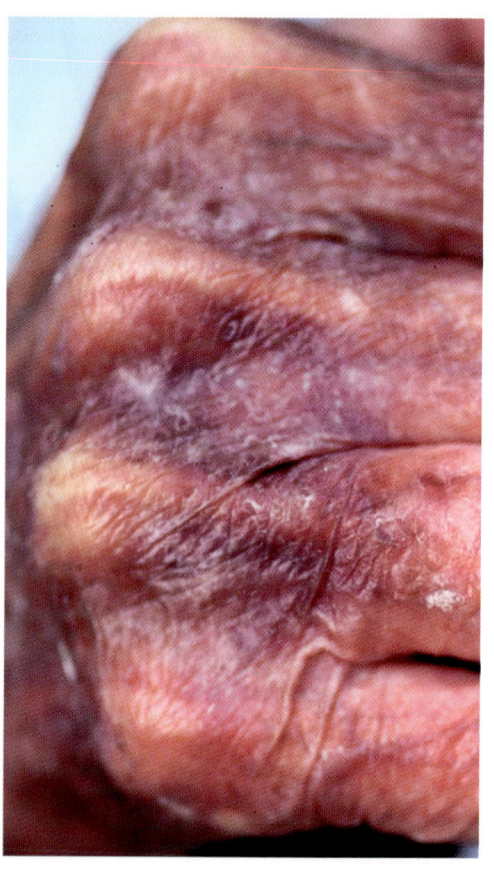

Hot and sweaty hands can indicate thyroid or glandular problems. Hot and dry hands can indicate kidney disorders or blood pressure. Cold hands can indicate circulatory problems, fever or shock. Cold, clammy patches suggest liver trouble and cold patches on the fingers (especially the left hand) show angina or something similar. Soft hands can be natural to the subject, but they can also indicate vegetarianism or pregnancy. Smooth satiny skin or very rough skin suggest thyroid problems.

HEALTH ON THE HANDS

Finger Nails

Finger nails are a terrific health indicator. Nails take around six to eight months to grow out from root to tip, so they show current or recent health and/or emotional problems.

Dents

Lateral dents mean an illness or shock during the previous six to eight months. This may be a dose of the flu (or something more serious) or an emotional upset. Weight loss can create dents.

Ridges

Longitudinal ridges show trouble with the bones and surrounding ligaments etc. One finger with one ridge shows that the subject will at some time have broken a bone, suffered from cartilage or ligament problem or perhaps had a slipped disc or something similar. If the ridge is on the thumb or index finger, the problem is likely to be in or close to the head area; if on the middle finger, the shoulders, spine, ribs or pelvis may have been broken; if on the ring finger, the arms and legs will have been hurt; and if on the little finger, the forearms, wrists, lower legs, ankles and feet will have suffered.

Older people may remember the days when a doctor checked for anaemia by pressing down on a finger nail and seeing how long it took for the pink colour to come back.

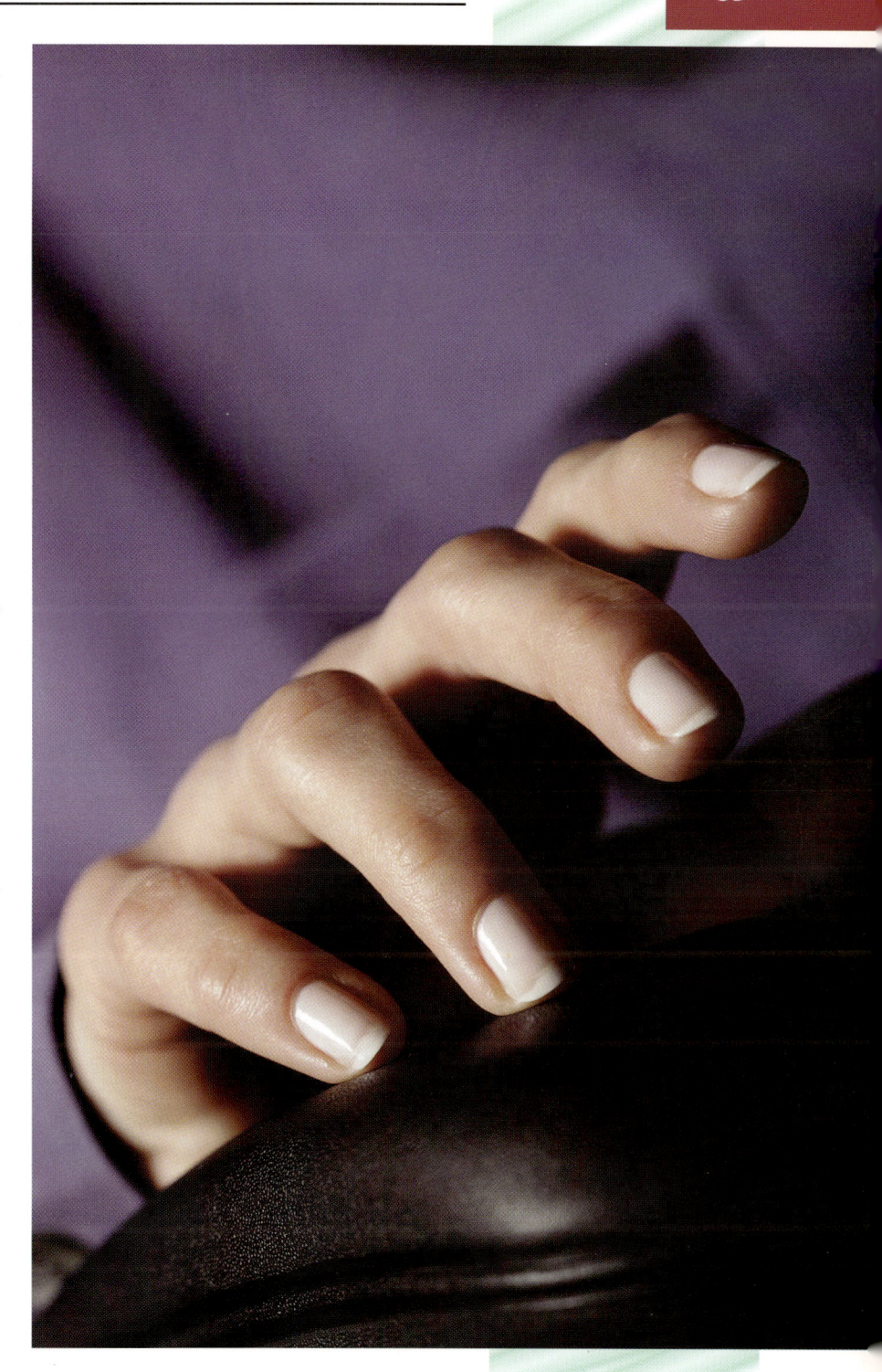

Above: nails are a terrific health indicator.

HEALTH ON THE HANDS

Right: nails can give clues to various conditions from spinal trouble to heart conditions and even vitamin deficiencies.

Here are a whole host of problems that can easily be spotted on the finger nails

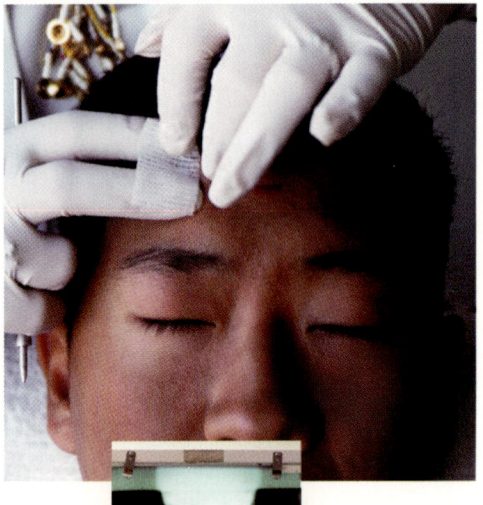

1. Tiny nails suggest stomach problems.

2. Watchglass or hippocratic nails are a surefire indicator of tuberculosis or lung cancer.

3. Slightly turned under nails also indicate lung problems.

4. Spoon-shaped nails show nutritional deficiencies or brain damage.

5. Pits denote psoriasis as does an overgrowth of skin around the nails.

6. White spots denote a shortage of vitamin A and D and calcium.

7. Dark patches signify candidiasis, the fungal infection.

8. If the moons change shape, heart trouble could be on the way.

9. Tunnel nails, especially on the little finger, suggest spinal problems.

HEALTH ON THE HANDS

Marks on the Hands

Other marks are difficult for a beginner to spot, but here are a few to look out for.

If skin ridge patterns are not so much ridges as "strings of pearls", the subject is ruining his health with alcohol and/or drugs.

If the area just above the heart line is hard to the touch and the skin ridge patterns pushed up, there is heart trouble.

If you push a person's fingers backwards and then see pits or blue colouring along the heart line under the mounts of Apollo and Mercury, there has been lung damage.

Pits or dots along the life line signify spinal trouble. The neck is towards the beginning of the line and the tail at the end.

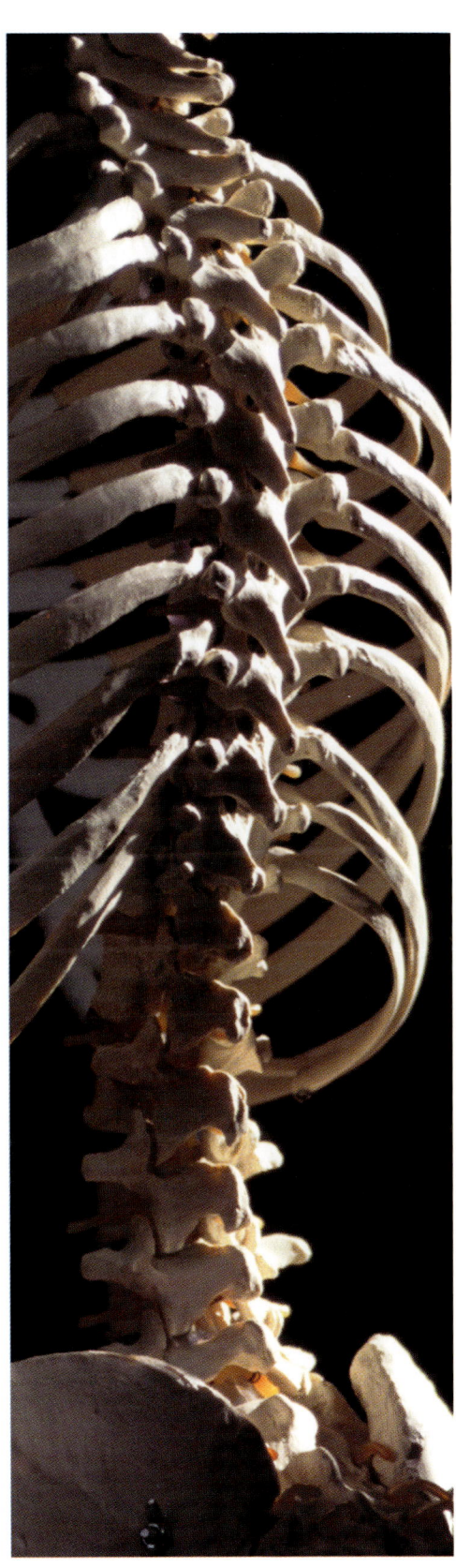

Left: pits along the life line indicate trouble with the spine.

Far left: skin ridge patterns can also indicate health problems due to alcohol or drugs.

HEALTH ON THE HANDS

Below: hip and leg problems show up as discoloration on forks at the end of a life line.

If the mount of Neptune is red or full of disjointed lines, the subject may have trouble in the reproductive area of the body. Redness here can also indicate pregnancy.

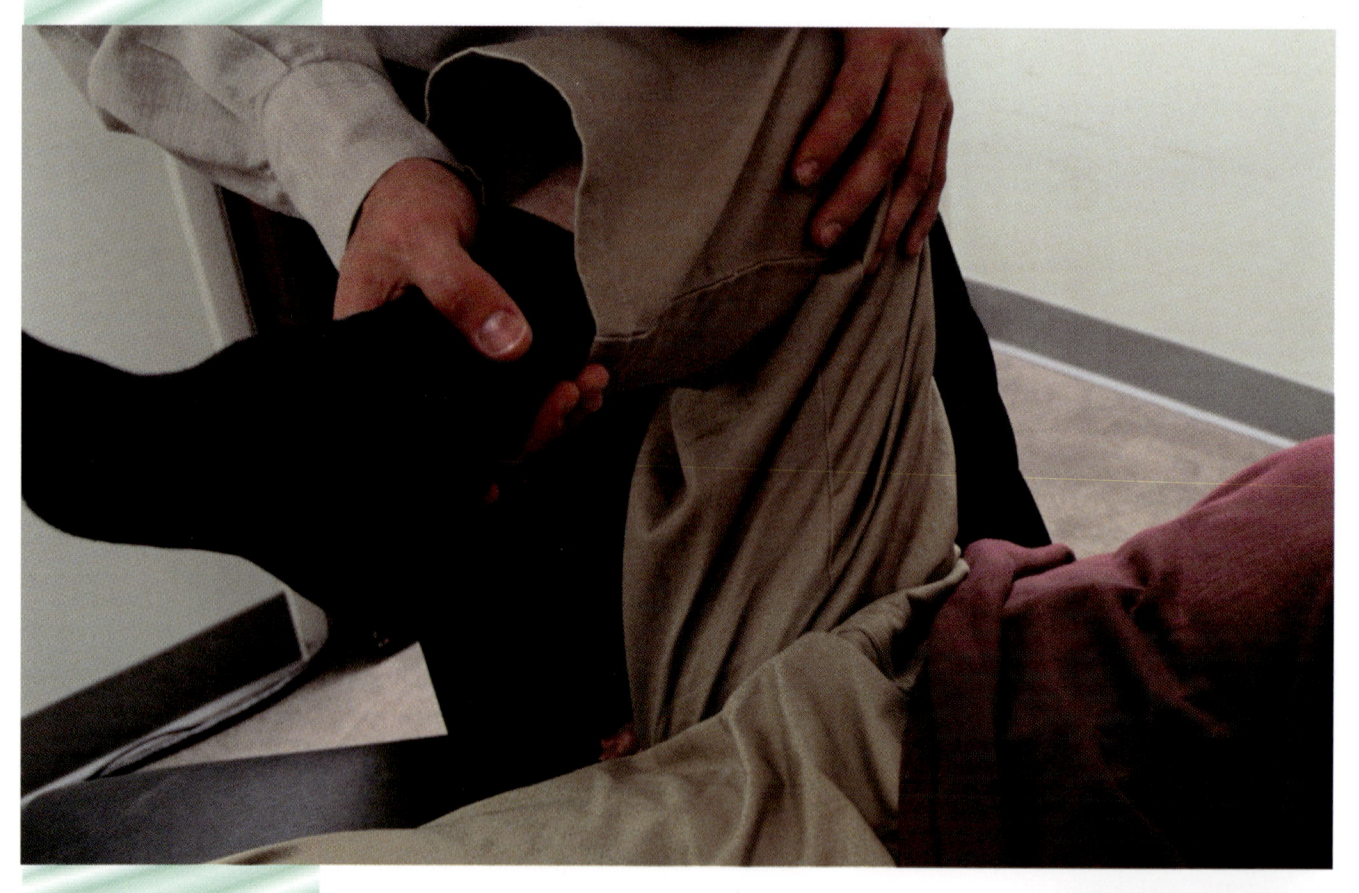

Right: redness on the mount of Neptune can be an indication of pregnancy.

If there is a fork at the end of the life line and if this is pitted or discoloured, there will be something wrong with the hips or legs.

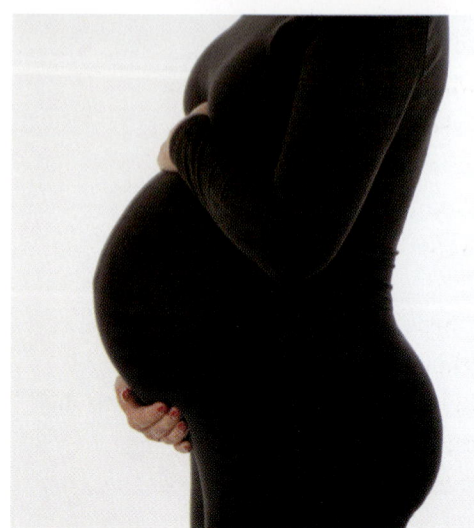

HEALTH ON THE HANDS

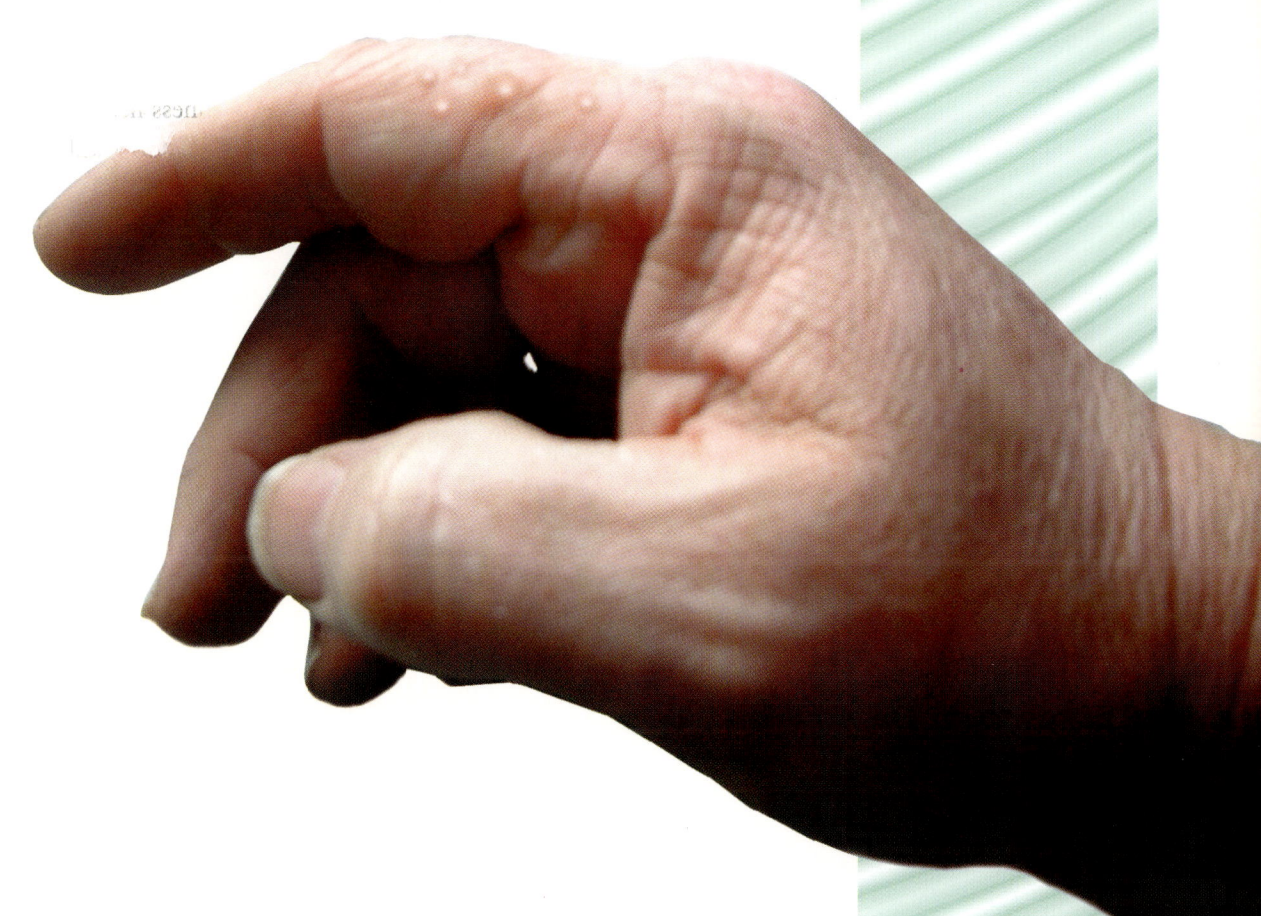

A grille is hard to spot. It looks like a cobweb or crosshatched effect that blots out some part of the hand. This indicates a severe shock to some part of the body. A couple of years ago, I became seriously ill with fibroids and then had a hysterectomy. A grille built up on the lower part of my hand while I was ill and then almost obliterated the lines for a while after my operation. It has gone now.

Small glassy warts on the radial (thumb) edge of the hand indicate tumours which may or may not be due to cancer. This effect can also be seen in tiny warts around the attachment lines.

Take care not to become paranoid about your health when you see a mark on your own hand and avoid making others worry, too. Stray marks come and go all the time, and hand colours change all the time. Any mark can show up for a short time, but if a mark or some kind of oddity persists (especially on the minor hand) then it is as well to get a thorough check-up, if only to put your mind at rest.

Above: small glassy warts along the radial edge of the hand can indicate tumours.

How to Make Hand Prints

Once you begin to become interested in hand reading, you will want to find a way of storing the information that you find or of keeping hand prints for research purposes. Lines change from time to time so a print that is dated and filed somewhere can always be fished out a couple of years later and checked against a person's hand. Another good reason for taking prints is that they show lines in graphic detail that might be difficult to see when looking at a palm. You can then look at your print with a magnifying glass at leisure, photocopy it onto paper or onto a transparency for an overhead projector or scan it into a computer.

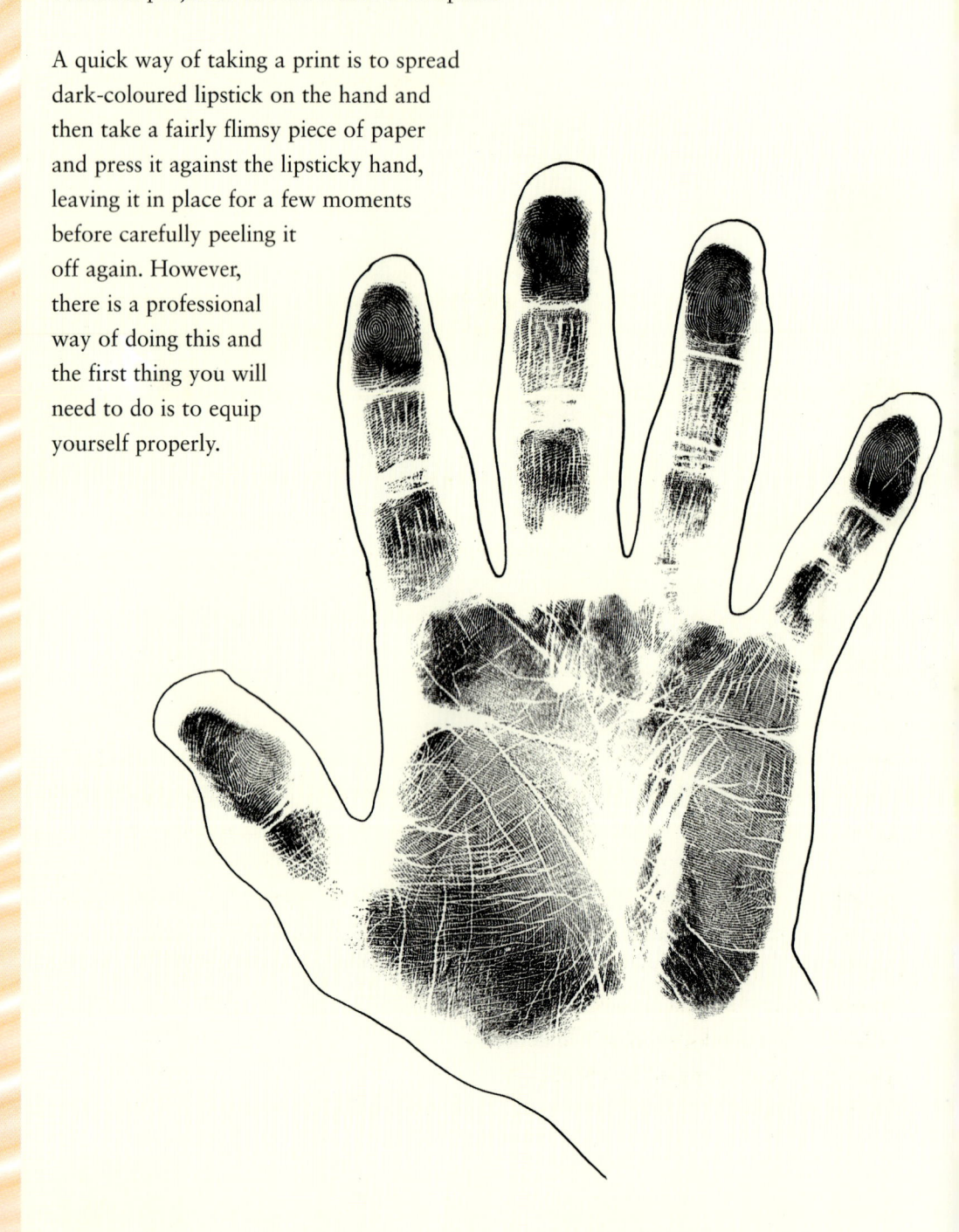

A quick way of taking a print is to spread dark-coloured lipstick on the hand and then take a fairly flimsy piece of paper and press it against the lipsticky hand, leaving it in place for a few moments before carefully peeling it off again. However, there is a professional way of doing this and the first thing you will need to do is to equip yourself properly.

HOW TO MAKE HAND PRINTS

You need to visit a shop that sells supplies for artists and buy a tube of water-based block printing colour which in the UK is marketed under the name of Rowney and sold through a company called Daler. This can be any dark colour, although black is probably the best. This comes in a tube which, when squeezed out, looks for all the world like black toothpaste. The fact that the ink is water-based means that it washes off the hands easily with soap and water and, if any of it gets on clothing, it will come out in the wash. Oil-based inks, especially finger-print ink, won't come off hands or clothes easily.

You also need to buy a paste-up roller (also from an art shop). This is a roller which is about two inches across and which has a rubber surface. You will need several sheets of A4 typing or photocopying paper and a number of sheets of soft kitchen paper, the kind you use to wipe up spills or as emergency table napkins. You also need an old plate or an old bathroom tile and a felt-tipped pen. Finally, you will need a volunteer to work on.

Equipment
Felt-tipped pen
Ceramic tile
Roller
Ink

HOW TO MAKE HAND PRINTS

1. Put several sheets of kitchen roll on top of each other to make a soft base. Take a couple more sheets and fold them in half so that the middle of your soft base is a little higher than the outside. This creates a slight ridge or mound. Then lay a couple of sheets of typing paper on the top.

3. Now ask your friend to hold their hand out straight and cover it with the ink. Place your friend's hand on the paper with the palm located over the slight mound in the middle. Don't press down on the hand or you will obliterate the print, but simply give the area where the fingers and thumb join the hand a bit of a press.

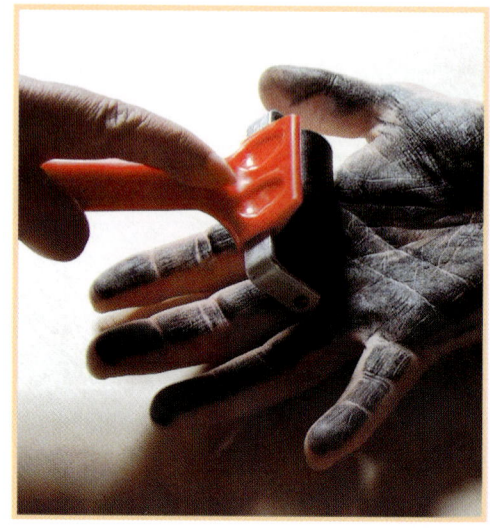

2. Squeeze a little of the ink onto your plate or tile, about the same amount as you would use for your teeth if it were toothpaste. Run the paste-up roller up and down in the ink until it is well covered.

HOW TO MAKE HAND PRINTS

4. Without lifting the hand from the paper, take the felt-tipped pen and draw round the hand. Don't angle the pen in around the fingers – just outline them. If you can't get between two fingers, don't try to push the pen in – just leave it.

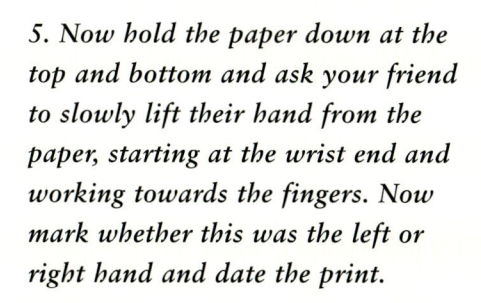

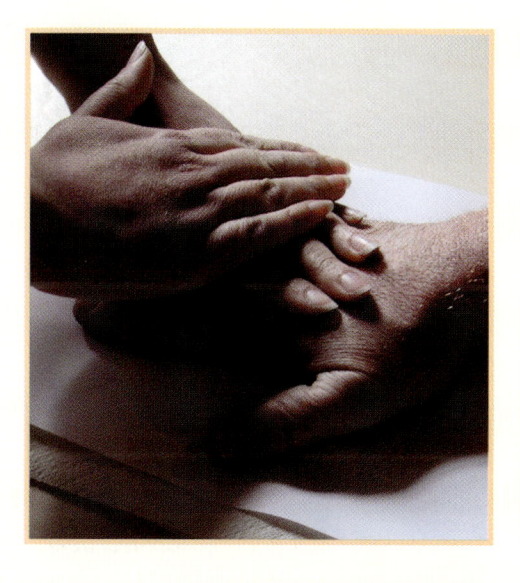

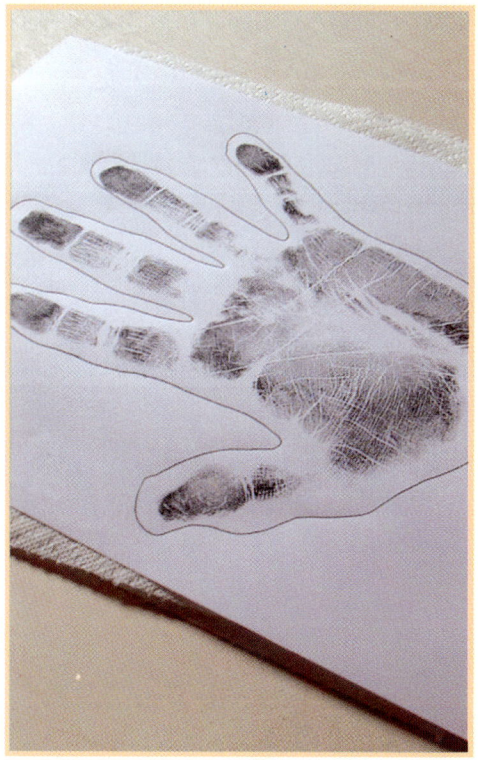

5. Now hold the paper down at the top and bottom and ask your friend to slowly lift their hand from the paper, starting at the wrist end and working towards the fingers. Now mark whether this was the left or right hand and date the print.

6. Do the same thing with your friend's other hand and then leave the prints to dry completely. Once they are dry, the best thing is to photocopy them and put the originals into one of those plastic pockets that fit into a ring-binder file.

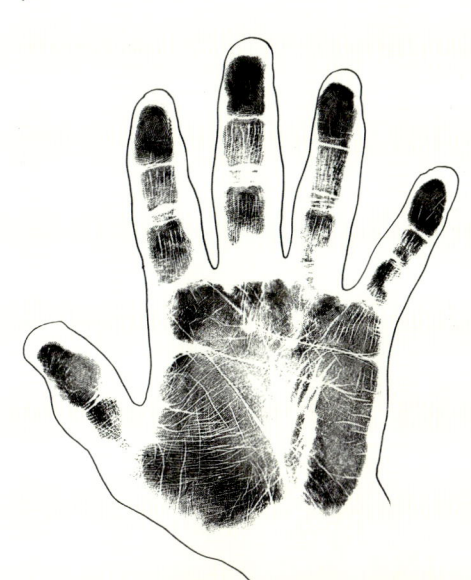

INDEX

A
achievement 25, 44
allergies 81
ambidexterity 9
anaemia 85
angle of rhythm 30
animals 61, 78
Apollo (ring) finger 14, 15, 18, 21, 25, 64, 71, 85
Apollo line 64, 71, 72–73
Apollo, mount of 24, 25, 72, 76, 77, 87
artistic talent 16, 18, 19, 21, 29, 72
attachment lines
    children 53, 60–63
    disturbances on 54
    doubled 56
    drooping 56
    health 74–75
    islands 54
    lines wandering into 57
    love 53
    multiple 54
    relationships 53–54
    rising 55
    shadowed 56
    V-shaped 57
    warts 89
    widow line 58

B
Bible, the 6
blood pressure 84
Bonaparte, Napoleon 6
bones 85
breast problems 52
broken heart 50
brothers 62–63
business 34, 42, 59, 70

C
calcium 86
cancer 52, 89
candidiasis 86
career 34, 38, 42, 46, 55–57, 70
cartilage 85
cat's cradle 40
cave paintings 6
change 10, 35, 46, 67
Cheiro 6
chest problems 52
child lines 60–63
children 14, 51, 56, 60–63, 68, 75
circulatory problems 84
clairvoyance 7, 74
colour 15, 84, 87, 89
communication 19, 26, 74, 75
computers 26, 40
confidence 21, 25
creativity 19, 23, 29, 72
cysts 52

D
danger 15
dementia 42
dents in nails 85
discoloration 7, 47, 84, 88
disturbances on lines 47, 54
divination 6
divorce 36
Down's Syndrome 11
dreams 29

E
education 38, 68
ego 17, 25
emotional problems 9, 85
energy 33

F
family 9, 15, 17, 18, 38, 53–63, 68, 70, 73, 82
fate line 57, 58, 64–71, 66, 67
fibroids 52
fighting ability 28
finance 15, 18
fingers
    arc setting 16
    cold patches 84
    fat 16
    fingerprints 20–21, 78, 91
    fingertips 13, 18, 19, 23
    flexible 13
    forefinger 14–15
    index – Jupiter 13, 17, 20, 21, 59, 71, 85
    knotty 16
    little – Mercury 14, 19, 21, 55, 59, 60, 64, 75, 85, 86
    long 12, 16
    middle – Saturn 14, 15, 17, 18, 21, 25, 64, 65, 71, 85
    nails 19, 85–86
    phalanxes 22
    politicians 13, 19
    ring – Apollo 14, 15, 18, 21, 25, 64, 71, 85
    short 16
    smooth 12, 16
    stumpy 16
    thin 16
    thumb 12, 14, 21–22, 24, 31, 67, 70, 72, 85, 89
friends 51, 57, 73, 82
fungal infection 86

G
girdle of Venus 58
glandular problems 84
grilles 76–77, 89
gypsies 6

H
Hamon, Count Louis 6
hands
actors' 12
angles 30
cold 84
colour 15, 84, 87, 89
conic 10, 11
cross 77
discoloration 7, 47, 84, 88
elementary 10, 11
empty 10
fat 12–13
fingers 16
flexible 12
full 10
health 84–89
hot and sweaty 84
knobbly 12
left 6, 9, 32, 93
loops 20, 78–79
major 9
marks 75, 76–83, 87–89
minor 9, 36, 66, 89
mixed 11
mounts 24–31
palms 7, 9–10, 13, 32–52, 76
percussion side 13, 20, 28, 60, 70, 75, 80
philosophic 11–12
politicians 13
pregnancy 84
prints 90–93
psychic 11
radial side 70, 72, 89
right 9, 32, 93
rounded 12
skin 78, 84, 87
smooth 12
soft 12, 13, 84
spatulate 11–12
square 11, 13
thumb 12, 14, 21–22, 24, 31
ulnar side 13, 20, 28, 60, 70, 75, 80
warts 15, 89
head injury 46
head line
    branched 44
    career 38, 57, 69
    chained 42
    curved 40, 72
    double 42
    forked 42, 44
    free 38
    islands 42, 46
    marks 76
    mystic cross 58
    secondary 44
    short 41
    sloping 41
    small secondary 44
    straight 40
    straight with sudden dip 41
    tied 38
    timing on the fate line 66
    travel 80, 82
    wavy 42
healing 74–75
health 9, 52, 84–89
health line 32, 56, 64
hearing problems 42
heart line
    Apollo line 64, 71, 72–73
    blue pits 52
    broken 50
    curved 51
    deep curved 48
    deep straight 48
    fate line 66–67, 69, 71
    forked 51
    fragmented 50
    islands 51, 52
    marks 75–77, 87
    marriage 53
    messy beginning 52
    mystic cross 58
    Saturn area 25
    shallow short 50
    small break or curve 51
    straight 49
    trailing lines 51
    travel 80
heart problems 84, 86, 87
hip problems 88
hippocratic nails 86
home life 18, 21, 27, 38, 67
humour 61, 78

I
idealism 25
illness 32, 76
imagination 29
imprisonment 46
independence 21
index (Jupiter) finger 13, 17, 20, 21, 59, 71, 85
inflammation 15
inheritance 72
introversion 12
islands 36, 42, 46, 51, 58, 60, 62, 66, 69, 82

J
Jupiter (index) finger 13, 17, 20, 21, 59, 71, 85
Jupiter, mount of 24, 25, 33, 72, 76–77
Jupiter, ring of 59
justice 28

K
kidney disorders 84
knotty knuckles 16

L
leadership 17

INDEX

left hand 6, 9, 32, 93
leg problems 88
life line
   Apollo line 72
   bars 36
   breaks 36
   broken 36
   career 34
   cat's cradle 40
   double 35
   energy 33
   fate line 68
   forked 34
   free 38
   health 32
   in relation to head line 38
   islands 36
   lower Mars 29
   marks 76–77
   mount of Venus 57
   mystic cross 58
   narrow 35
   pits 37
   tied 38
   travel 82, 87–88
ligaments 85
lines 32–52
lines
   Apollo 64, 71, 72–73
   attachment 53–58, 60–63, 74–75, 89
   bars 36, 46, 60, 70
   branching 44, 47, 69
   breaks 36, 46, 60, 62, 70, 72, 82
   cat's cradle 40
   chains 47
   child 60–63
   crosses 70
   disturbances 47, 54
   dots 47, 87
   fading 70
   falling 37
   fate 57, 58, 64–71
   forks 34, 42, 44, 51
   flaking effect 60
   frays 82
   head 38–47, 57, 58, 66, 69, 72, 76, 80, 82
   health 32, 56, 64
   heart 25, 48–53, 58, 66–67, 69, 71, 72, 75–77, 80, 87
   islands 36, 42, 46, 51, 58, 60, 62, 66, 69, 82
   jumps 70, 72
   life 29, 32–38, 40, 57, 58, 68, 72, 76–77, 82, 87–88
   Mercury 64, 74
   money-maker 72
   new home 36
   rising 37
   sibling 62–63
   Solomon 75
   stars 62, 70, 76–77, 83
   straight 61
   stray 68
   sun 64
   tassels 47
   tied 38
   trailing 51
   travel 80–83
   widow 55, 58
little (Mercury) finger 14, 19, 21, 55, 59, 60, 64, 75, 85, 86
liver problems 84
logic 21
loner 12, 59
loops 20, 61, 76–83
love 9, 14, 15, 18, 19, 27, 48, 53–63, 77
luck 72
Luna, mount of 24, 28, 68, 72, 76, 77, 81
lung problems 52, 86

M

major hand 9
marks 76–83, 87–89
marriage 53, 54, 57, 69
Mars, lower 24, 29
Mars, plain of 24, 29
Mars, upper 24, 28
materialism 29
maths 40
memory loop 78
Mercury (little) finger 14, 19, 21, 55, 59, 60, 64, 75, 85, 86
Mercury line 64, 74
Mercury, mount of 24, 26, 73, 74, 75, 87
Mercury, ring of 59
middle (Saturn) finger 14, 15, 17, 18, 21, 25, 64, 65, 71, 85
migraine 42
mind 38
minor hand 9
money 71, 72, 76
money-maker line 72
Moon, mount of the 24, 28, 68, 72, 76, 77, 81
moons of finger nails 86
mounts 24–31
music 16, 18, 27, 30–31
mystic cross 58

N

nails 19, 85–86
neck problems 37
Neptune, mount of 24, 29, 68, 88
new home line 36

O

obsession 74
old age 71, 72, 73

P

paganism 6
palmistry 7, 76
palms
   ambidexterity 9
   discoloration 7
   elementary 10
   empty hands 10
   fingers 16
   full hands 10
   lines 32–52
   major hand 9
   minor hand 9, 36, 66, 89
   random marks 7
   reading 7
   square 13
partners 54
partnership 53–63
passion 74
peacock's eye 20–21
percussion side of the hand 13, 20, 28, 60, 70, 75, 80
performing talent 72
personality 8, 9, 14
phalanxes 21
pits 37, 47, 86, 87
Pluto, mount of 24, 28
politicians 13, 19
possessions 27
possessiveness 27
practicality 18, 19
pregnancy 84, 88
prints 90–93
property 9, 15, 72
protection 76–77
psoriasis 86
psychic ability 28, 29, 74–75
Pythagoras 6

R

radial side of the hand 70, 72, 89
Rajah loop 78
rebelliousness 14
relationships 19, 48, 49, 54
reproduction 88
research 90
responsibility 10, 18
restriction 76–77
rhythm 30
ridges in nails 85
right hand 9, 32, 93
ring (Apollo) finger 14, 15, 18, 21, 25, 64, 71, 85
royalty 78

S

Saturn (middle) finger 14, 15, 17, 18, 21, 25, 64, 65, 71, 85
Saturn, mount of 24, 25, 73
Saturn, ring of 59
self-confidence 17
self-employed 70
selfishness 21
sensitivity 10, 12, 19, 58
serious intent loop 78
sex 19, 27, 33
shake test 14
shift work 13
shock 84
siblings 62–63
sight problems 42, 46
sisters 62
skin ridges 78, 84, 87
slipped disc 85
Solomon, line of 75
Solomon, ring of 59, 75
spinal problems 37, 85–87
spiritual mediums 29
spiritual protection 37
square marks 76–77
star marks 62, 70, 76–77, 83
striate 74–75
study 36, 58
style loop 78
success 25, 37, 44, 55, 59, 73
sun line 64

T

technology 26
temper 13
thumbs 12, 14, 21–22, 24, 31, 67, 70, 72, 85, 89
thyroid problems 84
timing 30, 66
training 36
trauma 9, 10
travel 9, 27, 28, 29, 77, 80–83
triangular marks 76–77
trident 72
trouble 10
tuberculosis 86
tumours 89
tunnel nails 86

U

ulnar loop 78–79
ulnar side of the hand 13, 20, 28, 60, 70, 75, 80

V

valleys 24–25
vegetarianism 84
Venus, mount of 24, 27, 57
versatility 42
vitamin deficiencies 86

W

warts 15, 89
watchglass nails 86
weight loss 85
white spots 86
whorls 20–21
widow line 55, 58
will power 21
windfall 77
wisdom 6, 25, 59
work 9, 34, 46, 59, 67, 70, 71, 76, 78, 82
Wright, Malcolm 50

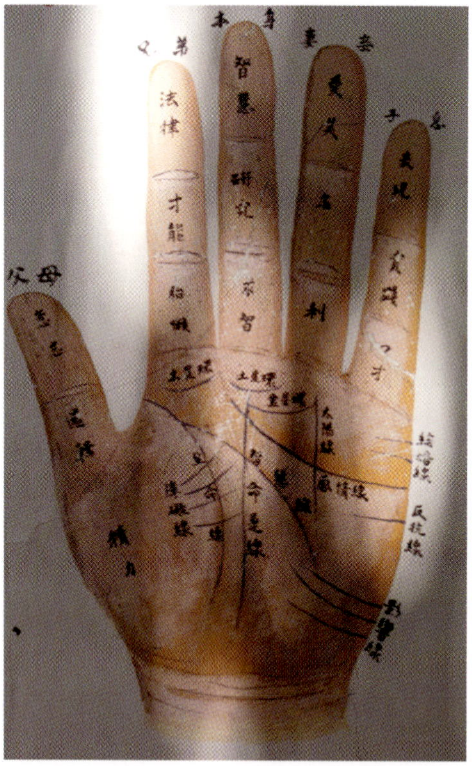